D0385071

READING
IN MEMORIAM

PRINCETON ESSAYS IN LITERATURE

For a complete list of titles in the series, see page 182.

READING
IN MEMORIAM

Timothy Peltason

PRINCETON UNIVERSITY PRESS

1985

Copyright © 1985 by Princeton University Press.
Published by Princeton University Press, 41 William Street,
Princeton, New Jersey 08540. In the United Kingdom:
Princeton University Press, Guildford, Surrey.

Library of Congress Cataloging in Publication Data will be
found on the last printed page of this book.

ISBN 0-691-06650-7

Publication of this book has been aided by a grant from the
Whitney Darrow Fund of Princeton University Press.

This book has been composed in Linotron Bulmer.

Clothbound editions of Princeton University Press books are
printed on acid-free paper, and binding materials are chosen
for strength and durability.

Printed in the United States of America by Princeton Univer-
sity Press, Princeton, New Jersey.

For my
mother and father

CONTENTS

PREFACE

I have described in this book my own experience as a reader of *In Memoriam* and tried to offer, after the first chapter, an exemplary and consecutive account of the poem as it is encountered in the act of reading. I have written for Tennysonians a more ambitious account of *In Memoriam* than any other I know, but I have also kept in mind readers who will use the index to find criticism and interpretation of individual lyrics. In my fondest and grandest dreams I am reaching out to an audience who will read around in my book as they have read around in the poem and end by reading more of both than they had intended: an audience of people who are interested in nineteenth- and twentieth-century poetry and like to talk about it, but for whom *In Memoriam* is not a very big or well-remembered feature of the landscape. One still finds little mention of Tennyson in the recent spate of books about the connection between Romantic and Modern poetry, and writers about poetry who are not Victorianists do not often look to him for poetic examples. Talk about Donne and Eliot has been succeeded by talk about Keats and Stevens or Shelley and Yeats, but Tennyson is still something of a missing link in most of the new literary histories. Harold Bloom is an exception, but he has written relatively little about Tennyson, nevertheless, and almost nothing about *In Memoriam*. The late Herbert Marshall McLuhan is another exception, but the suggestions of his 1951 essay, "Tennyson and Pictur-esque Poetry,"[1] about Tennyson's connections to modernism, have hardly been taken up. I have not redrawn the literary-historical map in this book, but by making my argument about *In Memoriam* a continuous argument *for* it, I have hoped to compel others to that labor.

Of course, I am neither brave nor original in admiring *In Memoriam*. There is at least one excellent book devoted to it, Alan Sinfield's *The Language of "In Memoriam,"* from 1971, as well as a full bibliography of articles and book chapters. There have been other handbooks and guides, too, including A. C. Bradley's *Commentary*, on which I have relied. But there is no book about *In Memoriam*, so far as I know, that attempts to read it consecutively and cumulatively, as I have, and there is surely room for more close and critical reading of individual lyrics. Reading through these lyrics over a period of years, I have thought that there was much to be gained from *In Memoriam*, and for it, by a critic who was willing to look longer and harder at the language than have other critics and to interrogate himself more closely as to the real source and quality of his own pleasure in it. And I have quoted freely from the poem, often transcribing whole lyrics, so that the reader may act immediately on my constant exhortation to look or to look again at one lyric or another. The quotations are not there to illustrate my critical points, but the other way around, and the reader who has-tens through them to get the gist of my argument—I often read this way myself—will be irritated and cheated. For my argument is sim-ply that *In Memoriam* is a better, stranger poem, and that it has a greater number of extraordinary lyrics in it, than most readers rec-ognize or remember. I trust that the readers who already agree with me and who know the poem better than I do will not mind seeing so much of it again.

I have called the book *Reading "In Memoriam,"* rather than *A Reading of "In Memoriam,"* because it does not offer a single, uni-fied interpretation of the whole poem, but rather a series of possible interpretations, tentative summaries or characterizations of the experience thus far. But I do not intend to make a theoretical statement about the possibility or desirability of such readings or to express any skepticism about the "reading" as a critical genre. Although many current theorists complain that we are flooded by explications and that criticism must find itself a new job, I do not find in the course of my own reading and teaching any overabundance of helpful guides to the poems and novels that I am puzzled by or eager to talk about. This book is full of readings, both of individual lyrics and of groups of lyrics, because in my own study of *In Memoriam*, it is the companionship and guidance of such readings that I have most often missed. There are any number of persuasive theories about the structure and movement of the poem, but these theories often tidy up the poem by sweeping under the rug of the unified whole the messiness of individual lyrics. I am sure that many readers and teachers of the poem and, indeed, many of the critics to whose theories of the whole I have just condescended, have had their own deep experience of the difficulty and value of these lyrics. But not much writing has come directly out of this experience, or so it seems to me, and I have tried in this book to err in a new direction by following closely the shifts and turns of the poem, even at the expense of the neatness of my own theories and arguments.

I wrote this book on a paid leave from Wellesley College, and I am grateful to the college for its generous support of junior faculty research. Many teachers, colleagues, and friends have taught me to read Tennyson and many others have read and helped to shape my writing about him. I am grateful to David Staines, Dwight Culler, Harold Bloom, Leslie Brisman, J. Hillis Miller, Bryan Tyson, Susan Cohen, William Cain, David Ferry, Margery Sabin, Arthur Gold, Robert Garis, Patrick Quinn, Gerald Bruns, and, particularly, to Herbert Tucker, with whom I have corresponded about Tennyson for many years, to James McMichael, who has read all my work with an affectionate seriousness for which I am affectionately grateful, to James Kincaid, who has so kindly and energetically supported my work and helped to get it into print, and to Christopher Ricks, who read the manuscript carefully and made many suggestions for improving it, some of which I was able to follow. For many years, Terry Tyler has been my colleague and dear friend and without the pleasure and instruction of his conversation, very little that I think or write would have been the same. Finally, I thank my wife Jan Harris, my aid and support in all things, for offering to this project her special skills as an amateur reader of Tennyson and a professional clinical psychologist.

READING
IN MEMORIAM

1

INTRODUCTION

In Memoriam was so quickly and surely established as the representative poem of its age and of its author that it must always have been difficult to appreciate its extravagance and its idiosyncrasy. Taken most often as the comfortably conventional expression of conventionally comfortable feelings, especially by those who have not read it recently or carefully, the poem is, in fact, very oddly made: each of its 700-odd stanzas the product of daunting and obvious formal constraint; all of its stanzas collected together into a large and uncertain form the rules of which nobody can quite discern. And it looks oddly made with good reason. Even for Tennyson, whose methods of composition were never straightforward or regular, the making of *In Memoriam* was a protracted and peculiar and largely a hidden business. Moreover, the individual lyrics just do not sound like most of Tennyson's previous poetry, so in recognizing them as Tennysonian, we must widen the reference of that adjective. The shortness of the lines; the almost laconic sharpness and concision of many of them; the trying out of ideas that must have seemed to Tennyson's earnest fellow Apostles, as well as to the harshly sensible critics of his first volumes, a bold striking out in new directions; the frankly autobiographical bearing of many of the lyrics: all of these signal Tennyson's possession of a new expressive idiom, an idiom that has arisen in response to new expressive needs and that reflects the exemplary strangeness of Tennyson's life and sensibility.

Begun in 1833 within a few weeks of Arthur Hallam's death, the sections of *In Memoriam* were written at many times and in many places over the next ten or fifteen years, but kept mostly out of sight while Tennyson revised the poems of his 1832 volume, wrote and rewrote the new poems that he would publish with his earlier work in 1842, wrote and then published *The Princess* in 1847, and lived the vagabond life that Robert Bernard Martin's recent biography has documented. Tennyson's father had died in 1831, and Hallam's death overturned the family once again, withdrawing suddenly the promise of some settlement in life, not just for Tennyson's sister Emily, who was engaged to marry Hallam, but for the whole family, whose connection to him must have seemed the connection to a world more securely and comfortingly ordinary than their own. In the seventeen years between Hallam's death and the publication of *In Memoriam* in 1850, Tennyson himself fell in and out of love with one woman, made and broke for ten years an engagement with another, worked on many different tasks, and lived and visited in many different inns and watering places and homes, none of them truly his own. And somewhere behind or between the narratable events of this period and the published poems, Tennyson was writing the different sections of *In Memoriam*, ranging widely in subject and mood, but keeping strictly to the four-line stanza and *a b b a* rhyme scheme that he had either chosen or fallen into as a way of binding together what he once considered calling his *Fragments of an Elegy*. Most of these fragments had probably been written by 1842, but they were not gathered together into the poem we now read until some time close to its official publication in May 1850, just a few weeks before Tennyson gathered together his private life as well, married Emily Sellwood, and settled at last into a home.

The finished poem records little of the external movement of this period of Tennyson's life, but registers finely and variously the psychic homelessness that accompanied it, the puzzled alternations of mood, the strange sense of starting over again with each new mood or moment, the persistent and frustrated search to put an end to this wandering among moods and to discover some stabilizing pattern in the history of recorded moments. For *In Memoriam* is exactly what Denis Donoghue has called all of Tennyson's poetry, "a Book of Moments,"[1] a book in which one moment, one lyric may continue from the last or may seem to replace it absolutely, leaving reader and poet together to confront the mysterious and unwilled changefulness of experience. The short sections of the poem, each divided into stanzas and each stanza closed in upon itself by rhyme, present to the reader discrete fragments of experience, momentary and present apprehensions. Even when individual lyrics look forward or back, as they regularly do, they are written from and for the present. The tentative organizations of experience achieved from within any moment can claim no final authority and must expose themselves to disruption or disproof in the moments that follow. And then these moments, too, present themselves to be assimilated, organized, understood.

As a long poem made up of short poems, *In Memoriam* naturally interests itself in the way that short structures build into longer ones, the relations of part to part and part to whole. But this formalistic language hardly evokes our experience of the poem, and the parts and wholes of *In Memoriam* are not empty forms. The investigation that the poem conducts into the relationship of parts and wholes is an investigation also of the principles of psychic change and of the possibility of psychic integrity, conducted from within the history of a single troubled and speculative consciousness. And when this consciousness takes on itself the burden of the exemplary, it casts the questioning of its own integrity in time as a questioning of the larger possibility of historical connection, where history is both what happens between one moment and the next and between the beginning of time and the end.

Mediating between these two extremes is the appropriate task of a poem whose form is the attempt to register great change incrementally and whose speaker is, in Tennyson's own words, "not always the author speaking of himself, but the voice of the human race speaking through him."[2] Tennyson earned the poet laureateship by writing *In Memoriam*—it is hard to imagine a reward more fitting or more truly deserved—and the poem repeatedly offers itself as a representative unit of human history, a model, for better or worse, of the individual life and the life of the species. Yet there is resistance as well as encouragement to this identification of the poet with his kind. The relationship of the part to the whole is antagonistic as well as constructive, and many individual lyrics subvert or challenge the process by which they are assimilated into a large and exemplary narrative, declaring the sovereignty of the moment and the absolute privacy and idiosyncrasy of the poet's experience. At the same time, however, this process of assimilation necessarily goes forward as one lyric, one moment follows another and as the poet continues to put his experience before us. Neither the poem nor its readers can renounce the difficult task of gathering things together and seeing them whole, of giving a name to the uncertain shapes of history, of human experience, of *In Memoriam*.

What the whole of *In Memoriam* teaches, we must stand outside any one of its parts to determine. And yet it is inside the poem, in the lyric-by-lyric experience of reading it, that we are given such carefully leading advice about how such determinations might be made. The parts of *In Memoriam*, both in their evocations of the moment and in their readings of one another, teach that history is Christian and redemptive, that it is evolutionary and progressive, that it is evolutionary and vicious, that it is meaningless and chaotic, that it is unreal, a travesty of the uniquely living moment. But whatever its models of human history, and even in its denials of history or of shared models for anything, the poem cannot help confronting the blank fact of change, a human mystery about which something must be said.

In section LXXVII, for instance, the poet thinks about the fate of his poem in history and the world.

> What hope is here for modern rhyme
> To him, who turns a musing eye
> On songs, and deeds, and lives, that lie
> Foreshorten'd in the tract of time?
>
> These mortal lullabies of pain
> May bind a book, may line a box,

> May serve to curl a maiden's locks;
> Or when a thousand moons shall wane
>
> A man upon a stall may find,
>   And, passing, turn the page that tells
>   A grief, then changed to something else,
> Sung by a long-forgotten mind.
>
> But what of that? My darken'd ways
>   Shall ring with music all the same;
>   To breathe my loss is more than fame,
> To utter love more sweet than praise.[3]

In the grimly reductive fantasy of the first two stanzas, history destroys the spirit, and the living, breathing language of the poet falls into the ludicrously material. The only resistance to this extreme materialism is in the extreme spiritualism of the last stanza, the defiant claim that value resides wholly in the self-sufficient act of the poet. He does not need history or an audience, but only the instantaneous fulfillment of his own expression. And lying between these two extremes is the poem's attractively modest and empirical description of itself; between the fantasy that it will have no worldly, historical career and the pretense that it needs none, the poem encounters its reader—the man browsing in the stall—and the inescapable fact that it is itself an action in time. Pages must be turned, grief changes.

"A grief, then changed to something else"; this perfectly captures the oddity and suddenness of transition from one section to the next of *In Memoriam*, or even from one line to the next within a section, as well as the deep mystery of the poet's spiritual regeneration. Mood succeeds mood according to some law or chance beyond the poet's control. The pressing concern then is to account for these changes, to ask how they come about and to ask if they constitute the coherent history of an integrated self or only the "wild and wandering cries" (Prologue) of a self in fragments. Or is there another form of coherence, another way to redeem these fragments

7

besides their absorption into a genetic history? These questions are both evaluative and analytic, questions about the success of Tennyson's effort to make a long poem out of short poems, as well as about the content and conduct of the poet's analysis of his own experience.

By "the poet" I do not mean the historical Tennyson, but the first person of *In Memoriam*, a figure who inhabits the poem, but also knows that he is creating it in words and meters: not Tennyson, but not just a character or "the speaker."[4] The evaluative question is not answered, but is at least asked more sympathetically and more searchingly, when we recognize in this way that Tennyson has gone before us and so arranged matters that the mourner's self-analysis is also a poet's self-criticism. More and more often as the poem moves forward, the poet is reading as he writes—"What words are these have fall'n from me?" (XVI)—and asking himself what coherent and speakable meaning can be extracted from the experiences that are arranged before him. And this presses us to ask, as both a critical and a philosophical question, what the very fact of arrangement means for the discrete value of single lyrics and single moments. Is the uniqueness and intensity of the moment betrayed or enhanced by its assimilation into a larger whole? Is *In Memoriam* more or less than the sum of its parts?

Much more, I think, and I have already started to say why in my remarks on the enriching appropriateness of the poem's structure to its subject matter. But I should address more explicitly the objections of those critics for whom the structure of the poem is inadequate to its large aims and irrelevant to an appreciation of its local excellences. And I should begin, as such critics generally do, with the apparent depreciation of this structure by Tennyson himself.

"The sections [of *In Memoriam*] were written at many different places," said Tennyson, "and as the phases of our intercourse came to my memory and suggested them. I did not write them with any view of weaving them into a whole, or for publication, until I found that I had written so many."[5] Though often cited as evidence that *In Memoriam* is rather a collection of fragments than a single, long poem, this remark might as easily describe the value that Tennyson attached to the work of weaving as a distinct creative activity. This weaving is not the province of "the poet," whose moods, like ours, seem to come unbidden and whose will exerts itself against the massy personifications that figure forth his conscious experience—Love, Grief, the Hours, Sorrow, Nature: not the province of "the poet," but of the author, whose offstage manipulations give the poem its structure. For many modern admirers of *In Memoriam*, this separation of creative faculties requires little discussion, and the poem successfully imitates, in T. S. Eliot's phrase, "the concentrated diary of a man confessing himself,"[6] or, another of Tennyson's provisional titles, *The Way of a Soul*. But for many others the separation between the writer of the individual lyrics and their arranger, between the poet and the author, is insistently there to be described, or to be regretted.

Christopher Ricks, offering the most acute and explicit of recent challenges to the unity of the poem, will not settle for "the unity and continuity of a diary" perceived by Eliot. "*The Way of a Soul*," says Ricks, "would indeed provide a graph, but a graph is not the same thing as an artistic unity."[7] Citing Charles Kingsley and Humphry House as allies, Ricks cannot find in *In Memoriam* the "conscious or organic method" or "single theme" that would unify the poem. The "links and cross-connections" among the sections do begin to weave the poem together, he acknowledges, but he does not think or make much of these and goes on to make an obscure, but apparently significant, distinction. "The Christmases, or the imagery of dark and light, of water and the human hand: these do much in the way of 'weaving them into a whole,' but it remains weaving, not growing or building." Ricks is distinguishing, I suppose, between an order imposed upon experience from without and an order that experience assumes, or convincingly seems to assume, in its own unforced unfolding. He wants *In Memoriam* to grow or to build as a piece of music builds, but not to be built—or woven—by an unseen hand. Alternatively, or perhaps in addition, Ricks and other critics of the poem's unity want a fuller and finer weaving of its parts, an arrangement that will show the relevance of each part to the whole and that will complete the exposition of a single, great theme. Either the poet or the author must exert greater control over his material and claim greater responsibility for the organization of the whole. But if it is not clear that woven things are less adequately made than things that grow or build, neither is it clear that "unity" is what *In Memoriam* must be shown to have in order to justify a decision to read and value it as a whole, long poem and not just as a collection of lyric hits and near misses. Long poems may be separable into parts, uneven in quality, and wayward in exposition—*In Memoriam* is all of these—and still require our attentiveness to the arranged relations between their parts and to the implicit and explicit claims to significance made by these arrangements.

It is not, then, a question of voting "yes" or "no" on the unity of *In Memoriam*. Ricks does not define, and I cannot define, "unity" in a way that makes the question of its mere presence or absence an interesting one. The question is how and how much to talk about *In Memoriam* and especially about the "links and cross-connections" that Ricks acknowledges, but spends no time on in his survey of the poem. The emphasis on local excellences results, in fact, in a serious undervaluing of individual lyrics, a failure to appreciate the extent to which lyrics and groups of lyrics serve one another as context or as subject matter. I am coming back around, of course, to an emphasis on the relations of part to part and part to whole, relations to which *In Memoriam*, in the felicity of its design, cannot help calling attention. The sections of *In Memoriam* do not just echo and remember one another, as Ricks's designedly dull catalogue of "links and cross-connections" suggests, but place in sequence and opposition an array of different arguments for feeling one way or another, and an array of self-sufficient moods that deny the place of argument in feeling, but whose sequence nevertheless constitutes an argument. This anteriority of mood to argument—the sense that even our experiences of inwardness may be passively discovered as much as willed or created or rationally chosen—is essential to the distinctively Tennysonian feel of *In Memoriam* and militates against attempts to explain the poet's progress as the working-through of a necessary and rational plan. And yet the poet does progress. A single ecstatic or grief-stricken part of *In Memoriam* may deny the authority of the whole, while the whole determines and limits the significance of any part and claims a separate authority for its own large movement from grief to affirmation. This tension between the part and the whole is the poem's continuous criticism of itself, and subsequent criticism properly acknowledges and builds upon it.

To read the parts of *In Memoriam* against the background of the whole, it is necessary, first, of course, to read them, and Ricks's criticisms might reasonably be directed at those accounts of the poem that spend more time on the elaborated unity of the whole than on the complexity and resistance of individual lyrics. The large structure of the poem can be overvalued and overemphasized by readings of the poem that accept its progress uncritically and that identify meaning with narrative content or, even more reductively, with narrative outcome. Such readings pause only briefly over the language of individual lyrics in retelling one version or another of the poet's story, a story in which these lyrics have only the value of incidents or illustrations. This plot-oriented criticism originates in a respect that I share for Tennyson's powers of construction and can reveal new patterns and correspondences in the poem, as well as solve in one way the problem of talking about a long poem in a limited space. But the emphasis upon plot serves Tennyson ill, even so, because it is not the separable plot of *In Memoriam* that can compel assent or admiration from the unconverted reader.

A narrative account of the poet's progress offers no new or persuasive versions of religious truth or religious experience, nothing that enables the doubtful reader to join the poet in his passage to comfort, whether we see that passage as having been accomplished by crisis and redemption or by gradual evolution. Both the gradualist and the apocalyptic visions of human experience in *In Memoriam* are too familiar to shake the reader into any new understanding, and none of the possible models of human history that the poem proposes can settle the human experience it documents into a single meaningful shape. But this limitation need not diminish the poem, as it will appear to do in any reading that has no time for the careful examination of individual lyrics. This is because Tennyson does not have to be a great and original arranger of the history of the person or the race in order for *In Memoriam* to be a great and original poem.

In Memoriam is a poem about many things, but especially about the arranging impulse in human consciousness, about the conditions under which we find ourselves pressed into making new sense of experience. One of its discoveries is precisely that the great arrangements of human life are not original or idiosyncratic, but historically and tribally sanctioned. For the poet, the impulse to arrange his life into some meaningful order is simultaneously the impulse to identify his own life with all other lives and with the course of human history. And so he finds his loss of Hallam analogous to the fall of man and looks forward to reunion with Hallam as he does to the "far-off divine event" that is the goal of the race. Or he finds his history of trials and sufferings analogous to the geological history of the planet or the evolution of the species. Or he finds the model for his own expression of grief and renewal in the forms of pastoral and romantic elegy. In this variety of ways, the poet experiences and interprets and calls into question the gathering up of his life into some larger order, which is at once the gathering up of fragments into the whole of *In Memoriam* and the emergence of the suffering poet as "the voice of the human race." And this experiencing and interpreting and calling into question happen in the way that consciousness happens, as a sequence of virtually present moments, each one of which is both inside and outside the history that it at once examines and enters.

In Memoriam comes to us in a form that insists upon both the autonomy and the connectedness of the individual moment, the individual lyric, and, as form finds its appropriate content, upon both the autonomy and the connectedness of the person. The interest and value of the poem do not lie in its elaborate or persuasive rendering of any one arrangement of the human world, but in its power both to realize and to examine the experience of a single consciousness as it wakens to and resists its exemplary condition, an apprehension at once of community and of mortality. And this interest and value will hardly survive translation into the terms of a critical overview. The experience is real, the examination subtle and rigorous, and the resistance credible only in the language of individual lyrics.

       I will turn in a few pages to the reading of these individual lyrics, to Tennyson's language as the justification for my own and as the only possible proving ground for my interpretation and my high evaluation of *In Memoriam*. But I have wanted to establish briefly the terms of my argument for the poem and especially for the artistic value of its special self-consciousness, for the ways in which it turns to account the oddity of its form and composition. The uncertain progress from one lyric to the next becomes an exemplary spiritual exercise, the work of weaving together discrete fragments becomes a poetic subject as well as a poetic problem, and this subject is dignified and enlarged by the experienced complexity of feeling that the poem offers. Self-reference is not an absolute good in poems, but when *In Memoriam* refers to itself it refers to significant human and poetic matters. The formalist critic who follows out these references does not abandon the great themes of the poem and of literary history, but examines them in the new ways that the poem itself makes possible.

Several of these great themes I have already touched upon in my suggestions that the productively troubled relationship of the part to the whole is at once the relationship of the moment to history, of consciousness to itself over time, and of the solitary self of the poet to all the different communities that he feels called upon to enter and to represent. The poem thus becomes an important event in, and an important commentary upon, Tennyson's own career—upon the notorious and intimately symbiotic relationship of "the two Tennysons"—and also upon literary history, particularly upon the history of Romanticism.

As a long poem made up of fragments, *In Memoriam* stands significantly between the long poems of the early nineteenth century and the self-conscious patchwork of such modern poems as *The Waste Land* and Pound's *Cantos*. The special interest of the poem as a link between the lyric practice of the early nineteenth and the early twentieth centuries is suggested by this passage from Robert Langbaum's *The Poetry of Experience*, one of the first of a distinguished and now various series of books to affirm the continuity of nineteenth- and twentieth-century poetry and the continuing dominance of Romanticism. Langbaum boldly names "the essential idea of Romanticism":

> That essential idea is . . . the doctrine of experience—the doctrine that the imaginative apprehension gained through immediate experience is primary and certain, whereas the analytic reflection that follows is secondary and problematical. The poetry of the nineteenth and twentieth centuries can thus be seen in connection as a poetry of experience—a poetry constructed upon the deliberate disequilibrium between experience and idea, a poetry which makes its statement not as an idea but as an experience from which one or more ideas can be extracted as problematical rationalizations.[8]

It is hard, as we read it, to take in and to test this assertion adequately, an assertion to whose explication Langbaum devotes the whole of an important and intelligent book. I would wish to demote "the" essential idea to an essential idea and to question the clear and sure hierarchy between primary and secondary, but I nevertheless think that Langbaum's formulation helps to bring into clearer relationship a great deal of obviously but obscurely connected material, from the first expressions of Romantic intuitionism and the quest for an "unmediated vision," to the prestige of "the objective correlative," to the latest assertion in poetry workshop or composition text of the superiority of "showing" to "telling." Langbaum's formulation helps to make clear another of the uses of *In Memoriam* and, especially, of the formal analysis of parts and wholes that follows the poem's reflections upon itself in the making. For it is precisely in the terms of Langbaum's formulation that Tennyson's works, especially *In Memoriam*, have often been depreciated as too much the mere statement of ideas. But *In Memoriam* is the book of intimately quotidian experience, too—"the concentrated diary of a man confessing himself"—and it may serve, if we will give full value to its experience and to its ideas and to their mutual criticism, as a profound meditation upon Langbaum's "essential idea" and as a central document in the history of Romanticism.

I should say something, too, about the great theme or themes that I will leave undiscussed, the themes of love and friendship. George Eliot said of *In Memoriam* that "the deepest significance of the poem is the sanctification of human love as a religion"[9] and Tennyson might well have agreed with her. But love and friendship are subjects of the poem only as they are idiosyncratically redefined by it. Although *In Memoriam* is obsessively concerned with a particular form of human relationship, this is not simply or precisely the relationship between loving friends. It is rather the relationship between a living friend and a dead one, between presence and absence, a relationship conducted over distance and through memory. Nor does memory do its work unaided in the poem. The poet does not commune with his absent friend in acts of pure introspection, but by reading the signs of his presence as they are secreted in landscapes, houses, and significant places, or as they are retained in his letters, or as they are absolutely created in imagination, with the poet writing stories of the history that never happened. Arthur Hallam himself is not a vivid presence, but a vivid absence, and the poet several times acknowledges his inability to commemorate his friend by depicting him or by reviving in narrative the experience of their friendship.

But this does not mean that Tennyson has followed his genius into solipsism or selfishness or that *In Memoriam* is a study of consciousness in isolation. It is, on the contrary, a poem about being in company, but particularly about the kind of company we are in when we read, about the company of the person who isn't there. Hallam is a "strange friend" (CXXIX) to the poet, a friend from the other side of a border or great divide. And the poet is a strange friend to his readers, of whose presence he becomes increasingly aware and whose companionship he solicits by offering his experience as representative.

A last great theme must be brought into view, if only to explain why I approach it so obliquely in the pages that follow. If *In Memoriam* is *a* great Romantic poem, it is surely *the* great agnostic poem, and God, as well as Hallam, is the absent friend whose uncertain signs the poet reads. But even the weirdly faithful agnosticism of the poem—the civil religion of the West for the last two centuries—looks more rigorous and can be looked at more rigorously through the analysis of poetic form, and this is the analysis that a close and responsive reading of *In Memoriam* forces on us. Very late in the poem, for instance, in section CXXVIII, the poet confronts the apparent chaos of human history and responds with an assertion of faith characteristic both in its tentativeness and in its yoking of artistic and cosmic order:

> No doubt vast eddies in the flood
>   Of onward time shall yet be made,
>   And throned races may degrade;
> Yet O ye mysteries of good,
>
> Wild Hours that fly with Hope and Fear,
>   If all your office had to do
>   With old results that looked like new;
> If this were all your mission here,

. . . .

Why then my scorn might well descend
On you and yours. I see in part
That all, as in some piece of art,
Is toil cöoperant to an end.

Although often quoted as evidence and illustration of Tennyson's vision of order, the closing assertion of this lyric is, in fact, abrupt and unsponsored and sends us back over the ground of the poet's faith in this and previous lyrics. The "part" of human history from which the poet has inferred his vision of order is apparently the course of mourning and recovery recorded in the poem. But "seeing in part" describes both a method of induction and its necessary limitation. The vision of order that has assisted in the poet's recovery is now inferred from it and then arbitrarily linked to the meaningful ordering of "some piece of art," a phrase that refers us inevitably to *In Memoriam* and to a consideration of its larger order. And the poet's relation to that order is neither innocent nor authoritative. On the one hand, he imposes an order by writing a quotable (and often-quoted) conclusion to his lyric that is itself an attempt at the justifying "end" that it describes. On the other hand, he can refer only uncertainly to "some piece of art"—a slightingly offhand phrase that works against itself by suggesting the fragmentary where we expect an image of exalted harmony. He makes this reference from inside a work of art whose structure he is confronting as experience. The providential hand of Tennyson the arranger he must take on faith, just as we decide to believe or not in Tennyson's arrangment of experience as truthfully or disinterestedly observed. Comparing an order discovered to an order created, Tennyson makes an assertion as arbitrary, as circular, as confessedly fallible, as temptingly and aesthetically "right" as the act of faith.

So Tennyson's faith in a larger order is at least partly a faith in the achieved wholeness of his own creation. And his celebrated failures of faith are challenges to that wholeness, appearing in what may be regarded as rebellions of the part from the whole. The

17

unique self and the unique moment rise up and refuse their membership in the redemptive systems of community and of history, and they do so in the space of memorable individual lyrics that refuse to cooperate toward the end of the Epilogue, that refuse to be read as preparations for "the one far-off divine event" to which the creation and the poem both move. T. S. Eliot's preference for Tennyson's doubt over his faith—"a poor thing" Eliot calls it—is well known and rightly influential, although it has surely influenced many people who hardly share Eliot's special reasons for deprecating a faith so carefully circumscribed and uncertainly professed. But Eliot was responding to what is there for every reader, to what James Kincaid has named as "the darkness and irresolution that remain suspended"[10] in the poem in spite of its closing affirmations. We can examine and enlarge upon Eliot's response by recognizing that Tennyson's faith is not a religious faith merely—not just a poor and vague version of the stricter faith that Eliot had discovered—but a faith in psychic integrity, in historical coherence, in the possibility of community. Eliot, from his special and interested point of view, could deplore this contamination of faith by historical and psychological and social experience, but these are the versions of Tennyson's faith that we have hardly outgrown and that we repose on far more unthinkingly than he does. We can still learn from a poem that defines and tests its faith in so many ways and that describes not just the mingled desire and reluctance of doubt to yield to faith, but also of the part to yield to the whole, of the unique self to become the voice of England, and of the moment to surrender its significance to some far-off divine event.

2

THE FIRST
MOVEMENTS
OF GRIEF

The juxtaposition of part and whole, of lyric intensity with the historical vision of the arranger, is the overwhelming structural fact of *In Memoriam*, emphasized in the poem's first gesture, in the placement of the Prologue in relationship to the lyrics that follow it. Tennyson gave no title to the stanzas "Strong Son of God, immortal Love," that appear in modern editions as the Prologue, but he clearly meant to set them apart from the numbered sequence of lyrics that composes the rest of the poem. Placed before even the title in the trial edition of the poem and marked off in all subsequent editions by the subscribed date "1849," these stanzas offer their secure and rounded assertions from some fixed point outside the partial and historical moments of the poet's experience within the poem. Written under the aspect of mid-century, if not of eternity, and from the end of sixteen years' mourning, the Prologue rises above the promptings of any particular occasion and presumes to address directly the God who merely overhears the poet's later questions and meditations. True, the God of the Prologue is embraced "by faith and faith alone," but the poet professes his faith clearly and forthrightly; it is a thing accomplished and not just aspired to, and it stands alone, confessing no indebtedness to the vulnerable and replaceable emotions of some one moment.

The Prologue not only presents itself as the summarizing culmination of many moments—the date emphasizes this—but presents as the object of its faith the complementary vision of a wholeness that triumphs over the partiality of any merely historical experience:

> Our little systems have their day;
> They have their day and cease to be:
> They are but broken lights of thee,
> And thou, O lord, art more than they.

On behalf of the species the poet decorously acknowledges the encompassing omnipotence of God. But then, in the last three stanzas of the Prologue, this public decorum slips oddly into the depreciation of the private experience of the poet, who sets against the vision of cosmic wholeness and harmony "the wild and wandering cries" of the poem to follow. From the heights of his magisterial opening stanzas, the author of the Prologue declines into the experiencing, struggling poet, and the reader is conducted into the poem as into the actual experience of a fragmented human history.

Directly in section I this movement is repeated, as if for emphasis, but also revalued, as the poet describes and emphatically rejects a model of history that would gather up the present moment into a redemptive order.

> I held it truth, with him who sings
> To one clear harp in divers tones,
> That men may rise on stepping-stones
> Of their dead selves to higher things.

> But who shall so forecast the years
> And find in loss a gain to match?
> Or reach a hand thro' time to catch
> The far-off interest of tears?

> Let Love clasp Grief lest both be drown'd,
> Let darkness keep her raven gloss:
> Ah, sweeter to be drunk with loss,
> To dance with death, to beat the ground,

Than that the victor Hours should scorn
The long result of love, and boast,
'Behold the man that loved and lost,
But all he was is overworn.'

Either the first or the third stanza of this densely worked lyric might be quoted out of context to illustrate one or another oversimple version of Tennyson's poetical character, the naively affirmative apostle of progress or the melodramatist of dark intensities. Reading the lyric whole and in context, we can appreciate not just the mutual criticism of these two attitudes, but also the care and the psychological shrewdness with which Tennyson both sets in motion the long drama of *In Memoriam* and expresses the emotions of a particular moment. The passionate refusal of consolation is a refusal to place the moment in history, to see and value in the present only its potential to become the future. Such a strategy would be at once too uncertain and too calculating, as the economic metaphor of the second stanza suggests, and the poet elects a full embrace of the present over the doctrine he once held or the far-off interest of tears—the personal and particular equivalent of the "far-off divine event" of the Epilogue—for which he might reach. In the clasp of Love and Grief, the poet discovers the image he needs of a constancy that will fight against all the forms of change and save him from the betrayal of progress.

For the man who has suffered already the awful change of his friend's death, the triumph of the "victor Hours" would be a second defeat at the hands of the same enemy. And from that closing image of the self "overworn" we must return to stanza one to glimpse for a moment the suggestion of grim exploitation in its image of "dead selves" used as stepping stones. The first stanza of section I places before us a tempting and idealized image of experience and of the poem itself, an image that will return subtly and diversely modified in the course of the poem. The resistance to this comforting image is not merely the sign of a pathologically extreme grief, not just an emotional disability that will go away in time for the happy ending, but a plausibly experienced challenge to the idea of spiritual progress that permanently qualifies our response to its images in the poem. Not the emotional blindness, but the clarity and undeniability of immediate experience.

And yet the histrionic intensity of this dance of death also criticizes itself. This is clearly a pitch of feeling that the poet will be unable to sustain, that he does not really sustain even through this lyric, with its second and fourth stanzas of questioning and speculation. The allusive connections to other sections of the poem also work against the exclusive cultivation of the emotions of the moment, preparing the ground for the repetitions of phrase and feeling in later sections that juxtapose one moment against another, setting up for reader and poet alike the central interpretive problem of *In Memoriam:* how to rationalize and to learn from the mysterious changes of thought and feeling that constitute experience. The intensity of resistance to change in this lyric testifies to its sovereign power, and the lyric is itself cast as an explanation and announcement of change, of the poet's abandonment of the truth he once held for the moment he now vows to hold.

Typically, this retreat into the moment is a retreat into the self as well, away from the communal emphasis of stanza one, which knew a truth about all men and shared it with another man. But although the poet makes what amounts to a pledge to be true to himself and seeks only the embrace between one of his emotions and another, he does so in a highly conventionalized language of public display. He leaves Goethe behind only to adopt the language of Satanic Romanticism, of Byron or Beddoes; the language of authentic feeling turns out to be the baldest and stagiest Romantic primitivism. But the poet is not too drunk with loss to produce the quieter language of stanzas two and four as well, to ask the questions of stanza two as if they might have answers and to look forward to the long result of love in genuine uncertainty. Changeable experience itself criticizes any attempts to control or to deny its progress, and the poet moves forward deliberately, feeling out his new circumstances in the world.

In one of his several explanations of the structure of *In Memoriam*, Tennyson told James Knowles that the poem fell into nine natural groups, the first two of which included sections I-VIII on the first experience of grief and sections IX-XX on the "fair ship" that bears Hallam's body from the Continent to its English grave. Through the lyrics of both of these groups, the poet tries to act on the resolve of section I by remaining fixed in the present and exploring the condition of the self in its contemporary relationships. Thus he writes the lyrics of direct address to the "Old Yew" (II), to "Sorrow" (III), to his own heart (IV), to the "Dark house" (VII), to the "Fair ship" (IX), and thus he examines the weather and the world, as in XI, "Calm is the morn" and XV, "Tonight the winds begin to rise," as a way of defining and expressing more precisely his situation. Even when perception yields to fancy, and the poet thinks of other mourners, as in sections VI and VIII, or flies in imagination to the ship at sea (XII) or pretends for a moment that Hallam is still alive (XIV), he is looking for ways to document the strangeness of present experience. He does not remember the past or look into the future or think at all about what it was to have Hallam alive, but concentrates his attention on the presence of absence, on the objectifications of emptiness and death, on Hallam as a phantom and as a corpse. The obsessive image is of holding fast, whether in the clasp of Love and Grief or the "Old Yew which graspest at the stones." Each of these images holds to the moment, resisting change, and also compensating the poet for the "hand that can be clasped no more" (VII), the truth no longer held.

But the poet will sooner or later have to confront the inconstancy of his own moods, the changes that inevitably overtake his expressions of constancy. When Tennyson said about *In Memoriam* that the sections of the poem came to him "as the phases of our intercourse suggested them," he described a drifting responsiveness to circumstance sharply at odds with the fixed resolve of section I. Even in the rearranged finality of the poem the sense of drifting persists, and one section follows another according to rules the poet does not make or understand. "I do but sing because I must, / And

pipe but as the linnets sing," says the poet of section XXI, disingen-
uously natural, but also honest about the extent to which he is
making do, responding as he can to the suggestions of the world
and the moods in which he finds himself.

Fixing upon the "Old Yew" of section II, the poet finds another
image of constancy, another way of mastering time, but in his fi-
delity to the image he is led away from the passionate intensity of
section I into some quite new quality of feeling.

> Old Yew, which graspest at the stones
>   That name the under-lying dead,
>   Thy fibres net the dreamless head,
> Thy roots are wrapt about the bones.
>
> The seasons bring the flower again,
>   And bring the firstling to the flock;
>   And in the dusk of thee, the clock
> Beats out the little lives of men.
>
> O not for thee the glow, the bloom,
>   Who changest not in any gale,
>   Nor branding summer suns avail
> To touch thy thousand years of gloom:
>
> And gazing on thee, sullen tree,
>   Sick for thy stubborn hardihood,
>   I seem to fail from out my blood
> And grow incorporate into thee.

This is one of the finest sections of *In Memoriam*, a justified
pathetic fallacy that neither forces nor follows the image, but meets
it in perfect adequacy. The perfect adequacy here is Tennyson's,
however, and not that of the poet, whose overconfident strength of
feeling has ebbed into this self-surrendering sickness. Placed beside
section I, this address to the "Old Yew" bears witness to the change-
fulness that the poet has hardly confronted, that he intends to defy
in his admiration for the stolidity of the tree. But stolidity is already

different from the wild grieving of section I, and the poet himself is neither stolid nor wild in these first movements of his grief, but nervously alive and attentive to the quality of his own experience.

He reaches down with the yew in the tactile precision of that first stanza, past the stones and names of the dead to "net the dreamless head"—an oddly loose and soft image—and then to wrap what we can only imagine as the reaching fingers of the tree around the bones that finally remain. But then, coming to this dead end of grief, the poet moves outward and upward to discover in the tree a form of transcendence. Overarching human time, the yew represents death, but it represents permanence and stability, too: not the blank end of every human history, but something securely outside the contingencies of all human history.

Grief cannot still the imagination—the poet refers in section LXXXV to "the imaginative woe, / That loved to handle spiritual strife"—and the poet in these early sections of *In Memoriam* re-imagines his grief in ways that keep pushing the self into new postures. From the deep fear that the self might be "overworn," the poet slips without acknowledgment into the yearning weakness of the last stanza of section II, a weakness that yearns after strength. In the curious play of experience from section to section, the poet then finds a kind of strength, following through upon and then rebelling against his own formulations. When Sorrow speaks, in section III, it is to take seriously the significance and the prominence of the yew, to call Nature a "phantom," a "hollow echo" of Sorrow itself. But the poet recoils from the figure that he has conjured up. He personifies the emotion, as he did the "Grief" of section I, conceding its autonomy, but also holding it outside himself, thinking of it as something that he might choose, or not:

> And shall I take a thing so blind,
>   Embrace her as my natural good;
>   Or crush her, like a vice of blood,
> Upon the threshold of the mind?

We think we know the answer to this question, that the balance has shifted, and that the poet's instinctive sense of "natural good" rises up in strength against the surrender of Nature to Sorrow. Section IV continues in this resistance to Sorrow, beginning with a surrender of the will—"To Sleep I give my powers away; / My will is bondsman to the dark"—but ending in a triumphant awakening: "With morning wakes the will, and cries, / 'Thou shalt not be the fool of loss.' " But of course, the shifting and changing of moods has just begun, and sections III and IV do not so much answer or move beyond the preceding sections as add to them other ways of experiencing the present tense of grief. As section follows section, the poet implicitly and explicitly challenges and modifies his own accounts of experience, matching one mood against another, discovering that different moods might start from the same resolution or go by the same name, pressing us to discover that similar diagrams of human experience may be inferred from what are, in fact, quite different experiences. Thus, sections III and IV, which qualify our response to what has preceded them, leave themselves open to revaluation. Section III does end with a question, after all, and not an assertion. And the will that awakens in section IV is oddly unwilled, something that the poet discovers in himself, but does not seem to control, so that the poem opens out into a future that it can only begin to predict.

The future is there, at least, for the last stanza of section IV, the poet does look forward, and poet and reader together learn from the accretion of lyric moments that time has not stopped after all. The attempt to live in a perpetual present of grief is inevitably frustrated by the mysterious forward momentum of consciousness. But this movement is not all in the direction of the future or of sure healing. There is a pull toward the past, too, resisted far more frequently than we expect it to be in Tennyson, but powerful, nevertheless. Love may strive to remain the same, but the tragic difference of the present from the past cannot be suppressed. In section VII, for instance, singled out for praise by T. S. Eliot in his essay on *In Memoriam*, the poet continues to place himself and his grief in relation to the objects of the world, but these objects are haunted, and he cannot keep himself from the past.

> Dark house, by which once more I stand
> Here in the long unlovely street,
> Doors, where my heart was used to beat
> So quickly, waiting for a hand,
>
> A hand that can be clasp'd no more—
> Behold me, for I cannot sleep,
> And like a guilty thing I creep
> At earliest morning to the door.
>
> He is not here; but far away
> The noise of life begins again,
> And ghastly thro' the drizzling rain
> On the bald street breaks the blank day.

The brittleness of that last line, which mimics the feel of a day and a life that are breaking not into light, but into pieces; the obtrusive, but not excessive, bleakness of diction; the quick, devastating reduction of life to "noise" and self to "thing"; these evoke desolation of spirit with a skill that clearly merits Eliot's praise. But I am especially interested in the sudden prominence of the past tense in the recollection that intrudes between the opening address and its completing clause "Behold me." The first two lines set the scene, but then the poet stalls and repeats his address. The crack opened by the "once more" of line one widens abruptly at line three into an abyss, and the poet falls into memory. His heart seems to beat quickly even now, but that is not enough, for the object of its desire has vanished. The repetition of "hand" in lines 4 and 5 reveals the jerky, involuntary quality of these reflections, one thought suggesting the next, but also draws the sequence up short against the blank realization of loss. These thoughts have been inadvertent, an intrusion into the planned address, as the closing punctuation of line 5 indicates. The third stanza more calmly confronts Hallam's absence, but the ambiguous wording of the first line, which seems at first a continuous, complete thought, resolutely makes of that absence a fact of space and not of time. The poem has regained its dismal poise, and the coming of day brings no change of mood.

In the first confusions of his grief, the poet has sought to make a home of the changeless, grief-stricken present, to hold himself steady in his relation to the physical and emotional circumstances of the moment. Arthur Hallam died on September 15, 1833, but he was not finally buried in England until January 3, 1834, and the first twenty sections of *In Memoriam* seem to correspond to this long first phase of grief, between the first shocking news and the ritual closure of the funeral. Starting at section IX, the poet follows the progress of his friend's body back to England, and his anxiety for the "Fair ship" that bears it will seem excessive only if we cannot appreciate the poet's need for emotional anchorage, his fear of existential and emotional freedom. Such a freedom courts the twin dangers of despair and of recovery, threatens to generalize grief into a confrontation with the absurdity of the universe—a confrontation refused in section III and deferred until later in the poem—or to heal grief and thus to commit the sin of disloyalty.

The poet himself recognizes the folly of his attachment to his friend's body and grave—we are "fools of habit," he admits in section X, for preferring a "rest beneath the clover sod" to this strangely and vividly imagined burial at sea:

> . . . the roaring wells
> Should gulf him fathom-deep in brine
> And hands so often clasp'd in mine,
> Should toss with tangle and with shells.

But habits, rituals, repetitions are powerful and steadying, and the poet's obsessive attachment to certain images and issues is a source both of poetic power and of emotional steadiness. The "hand that can be clasp'd no more" is evoked for us again here—the poet's clasping to this image is notorious. And the idea of watery burial has already acquired a weird potency in the image that rises out of the otherwise drably, if intentionally, commonplace list of bereavements in section VI:

> O mother, praying God will save
> Thy sailor,—while thy head is bow'd,
> His heavy-shotted hammock-shroud
> Drops in his vast and wandering grave.

The irony is heavy here, but the last two lines come alive, and especially the "vast and wandering grave," an image that mocks the desire of the poet to cling to his dead friend. Not even a yew tree could attach itself to the sea. When even the grave wanders, how can the mourner hold fast?

He can try, as the poet of sections IX-XVII does, to attach his imagination to the wandering grave of his friend at sea, to follow the fair ship solicitously to port. But such a task will hardly quiet the play of fancy—Tennyson's word for it, used four times in this sequence—which carries the poet out to the ship in section XII, but then cannot keep itself to the sober facts and must imagine the body away or bring it back to life in sections XIII and XIV. These strange fancies, conveying the poet's shocked sense that anything would be less strange than the truth, do not yet betray the dead, but they are distractions from the proper business of grieving. And in three more considerable lyrics, sections XI, XV, and XVI, the poet does consider a kind of betrayal, the betrayal by changeable sorrow of itself. Ostensibly concerned for the safety of the ship at sea, the poet keeps watch more nervously on the inconstancy of his own imagination, on the troubled relationship of inner to outer weather. The poet writes and then reflects upon a pair of Romantic nature lyrics, modifying the received material of the form to suit his needs, complicating the relationship of mind and world by attempting to hold

29

both in relationship to the dead body of his beloved friend. In the ominously repeated calm of section XI, these three elements just hold together:

> Calm is the morn without a sound,
>   Calm as to suit a calmer grief,
>   And only thro' the faded leaf
> The chestnut pattering to the ground:
>
> Calm and deep peace on this high wold,
>   And on these dews that drench the furze,
>   And all the silvery gossamers
> That twinkle into green and gold:
>
> Calm and still light on yon great plain
>   That sweeps with all its autumn bowers,
>   And crowded farms and lessening towers,
> To mingle with the bounding main:
>
> Calm and deep peace in this wide air,
>   These leaves that redden to the fall;
>   And in my heart, if calm at all,
> If any calm, a calm despair:
>
> Calm on the seas, and silver sleep,
>   And waves that sway themselves in rest,
>   And dead calm in that noble breast
> Which heaves but with the heaving deep.

A lot of work is done here by one word, and it is by repeating that word steadily and by attending closely to the still and spacious scene before him that the poet achieves the calmer grief called for by word and scene both.[1] But the harsher wording of "calm despair" contains a shudder, a dangerous wavering felt in the repeated "if" clauses of lines 15 and 16. The "dead calm" of the last stanza so qualifies the key word that the calm surface of the poem is almost broken. But this is not the clear subversion of irony, and the word has not suddenly turned against itself and against the lovely serenity of the opening. There has rather been a gradual evolution of mood, a steady following through of the implications of a calm stillness and of the implications, too, of a sympathy with nature that attains its ominous completion in the repetitions of the final line.

The fuller and more exciting break of feeling comes in section XV. There is a big change in the weather, the west wind is rising, and the poet responds with a lyric of Shelleyan speed and power.

> To-night the winds begin to rise
> And roar from yonder dropping day:
> The last red leaf is whirl'd away,
> The rooks are blown about the skies;
>
> The forest crack'd, the waters curl'd,
> The cattle huddled on the lea;
> And wildly dash'd on tower and tree
> The sunbeam strikes along the world:
>
> And but for fancies, which aver
> That all thy motions gently pass
> Athwart a plane of molten glass,
> I scarce could brook the strain and stir
>
> That makes the barren branches loud;
> And but for fear it is not so,
> The wild unrest that lives in woe
> Would dote and pore on yonder cloud
>
> That rises upward always higher,
> And onward drags a labouring breast,
> And topples round the dreary west,
> A looming bastion fringed with fire.

Even before the unrestful poet has begun to follow his fancies, the descriptive language of the first two stanzas bears witness to decisive and irresistible change. The first line names the beginning of something and the third notices the end of a process of change that was indefinitely suspended in the imagery of section XI. The "leaves that redden to the fall" have by now completed their change and fallen, and the last of them is swept away by a wind that is, like Shelley's West wind, the exclusive agent of all activity. The rooks cannot fly themselves, but are blown about the skies. Land and air and sea are acted upon until the description of wild, natural activity culminates strangely in an image of light: "And wildly dash'd on tower and tree / The sunbeam strikes along the world." The first line belongs clearly to the frenzy of the storm and seems to affirm its continued sovereignty, but in the second the sunbeam asserts itself unexpectedly and alters the scene. Although it "strikes," still a sudden and violent action, the sunbeam seems for a moment to counter the glowering storm and to irradiate the world just at the moment of impending darkness. And as soon as the sunbeam has struck, the poem changes direction, and the poet's imagination emerges in response to the stormy scene.

The poet tries first the simple fancy that does not engage the storm, but turns from it. The address to the ship—"all thy motions"—accents such a turn, for the poet now faces, at least in fancy, toward the east and the approaching ship. But this turning does not protect him from the distress that enters the poem anyway in the conditional clause of lines 12 and 13. The poet balances his fear for the ship against his fancy and then balances both against the crucial and independent flight of feeling that takes up the final six lines of the lyric, a flight that is anchored by the conditional verb, but that carries the poet up and away, nevertheless, with "yonder cloud." In the branching clauses of the last three stanzas, the poem has it all ways at once, and imaginative and emotional energy is at once expended and contained in a manner that is the characteristic strength of *In Memoriam*.

Curiously at issue, as in earlier sections, is the poet's loyalty to his dead friend. The "wild unrest that lives in woe" is not just the perturbation of spirit that naturally accompanies grief, but something that presses further and that may lift grief out of itself, the promiscuously "imaginative woe" of section LXXXV. A. C. Bradley takes the last lines of the poem to mean that the poet's unrest would "sympathize"[2] with the storm were it not for his fears for the ship. Yet doting and poring go beyond sympathy. In his heightened attentiveness to natural appearances, the poet discovers a restorative human truth, and the cloud that "rises upward always higher" is a renewed image of the spiritual progress that the poet has earlier resisted, at once humanized and impeded by its "labouring breast." But although the struggle is not easy or certain of outcome and the cloud will eventually "topple," it remains still "a looming bastion fringed with fire," an image of light as well as darkness, a cloud with a lining of gold. Teased out of his obsession with the safety of the returning ship, if only for a wild moment, the poet discovers in the scene before him a luminous promise and section XV looks for a moment like an account of the healing and reconciling powers of the imagination, an account on which this extraordinary passage from Coleridge's letters might serve as a shrewd gloss:

> We imagine the presence of what we desire in the very act of regretting its absence, nay *in order* to regret it the more livelily; but while, with a strange wilfulness, we are thus engendering grief on grief, nature makes use of the product to cheat us into comfort and exertion. The positive shapings, though but of the fancy, will sooner or later displace the mere knowledge of the negative. All activity is in itself pleasure; and according to the nature, powers, and previous habits of the sufferer, the activity of the fancy will call the other faculties of the soul into action.[3]

This beautifully describes the collusion of nature and imagination that cheats the poet in the first sections of *In Memoriam* into change, if not quite into comfort, and that produces in section XV the closing image of spiritual progress. But as another unexpected feature of that rising cloud suggests and as the rest of *In Memoriam* confirms, the poet has hardly left off grieving in order to follow nature. He is not elsewhere compelled to choose between nature and grief, as they are joined under the sign of the yew tree, or between nature and Hallam, who are intermingled in the triumphant closing sections of the poem. Tennyson nowhere consults nature as if it were the autonomous author of human or religious truths. *In Memoriam* notoriously struggles, in fact, to separate natural from religious speculations, lest the image of a loving God be shattered by the spectre of "Nature, red in tooth and claw" (LVI). When the poet reports in section CXXIV that "I found Him not in world or sun, / Or eagle's wing or insect's eye," he is stating the consistent anti-Paleyan philosophy of the poem and of its author, for whom human meanings do not reside in nature, but are imposed on it by acts of imagination.

The "nature" of Coleridge's meditation emanated from no landscape and was arguably a human nature alone, but it acted still with the kindly solicitude of some loving higher power. Returning to section XV and to the more relevant Shelleyan heritage of that lyric, it is evident that the power honored there is a power of solitary resistance. The struggling cloud, which will "topple round the dreary west," must struggle because it moves against the wind, back into the western sky out of which the wind roared in line two. Tennyson was a scrupulously faithful recorder of natural detail, indignant when Ruskin used a line from *Maud* as an example of the pathetic fallacy[4], and it would be dangerous to assume that he merely inserted this meteorologically doubtful cloud into the scene or changed its bearing to suit his meaning. But he has undoubtedly turned into the wind and, in the focused intensity of his doting and poring on that one cloud, has imaginatively turned the storm against itself. In section XI, the poet held together with difficulty the calm of the morning and his own calm despair and the dead calm of the friend to whom his thoughts still returned. But in section XV's scene of wild unrest, the three elements pull apart, and the poet's own wild unrest asserts its autonomy in spite of all efforts to contain it. The winds rose earlier, and now the poet fixes upon the single cloud that rises against them. The imagination may be a power of opposition and division, too, carrying the poet away from himself in time and toward an identity that is merely potential in the present.

I have referred repeatedly to Shelley's "Ode to the West Wind" as a possible source for the weather of section XV and of a plot that rises through that weather to imaginative assertion. But the important differences between the two poems help to define the peculiarly Tennysonian strength of *In Memoriam*. Shelley's poem ends in unrestrained triumph, the poet turning the wind to account by taking on its power as his own. For Harold Bloom, Shelley's strong finish is a defense against "Wordsworth's account of imaginative loss being transformed into experiential gain."[5] The poet will not surrender or subordinate his power to the powers of nature, even if these are part of a necessary and regenerative cycle.

But for *In Memoriam* the terms are reversed, and the poet resists a transformation of experiential loss into imaginative gain. He does not wish to be cured of his grief or to find it too readily turned into triumphant poetry, and his guilty resistance to imaginative progress is felt in section XV as the drag of the "labouring breast," the downward pull of the death ship to which his thoughts are anchored. The difficulty is not just internal and psychological, however, and the poet also faces the resistance of the storm itself. Even when he has for a moment broken free of morbid attachment, he imagines his freedom as effortful and uncertain. The wild unrest of the storm provokes the poet into beginning a natural movement out of grief, but the sweeping west wind of autumn also represents the mutability and mortality of all natural things, the deathly facts of nature that the poet is only beginning to face and against which his obsessive grief has been a defense.

The west wind threatened death to Shelley, too, of course, but the poet of section XV, unlike Shelley, has no triumph to record, no sure sense of the course that he must pursue. He stands at what Bloom would likely call a less advanced stage of his imaginative career and makes what Bloom would surely call a weaker statement. But it is possible to see the poet's uncertainty in section XV as humanly broadening, as providing a psychological and social context for the single-purposed act of the imagination. The cautious watchfulness of *In Memoriam* immediately contains and criticizes any rising sublimity, but it also keeps calling into question, as Tennyson's poetry always has, the independent authority of any power outside the self—of nature, of the community, of a God who may or may not be there, of the dead friend the precise nature of whose existence is so urgently uncertain. The intensities of feeling that master every natural or social or historical context are also mastered by them, placed as but one moment in a series. This is yet another way in which the form of *In Memoriam* perfectly matches its persistent psychology of agnosticism and perfectly expresses the dilemma of a mind that knows and feels all the arguments both for and against the existence of an external and determining power.

This relentless self-checking tendency is manifested most clearly in the shifts from one lyric to the next. Section XVI immediately stalls the imaginative flight of section XV, seeking to place it in context and to assimilate and understand it. This means that the poet of section XVI must now see that he has begun to change with the changing season, to enter the communities of nature and time. But it also marks the beginning of explicit reflection on his poetic enterprise, an implicit acknowledgment that his own most urgent subject is himself.

> What words are these have fall'n from me?
>> Can calm despair and wild unrest
>> Be tenants of a single breast,
> Or sorrow such a changeling be?
>
> Or doth she only seem to take
>> The touch of change in calm or storm;
>> But knows no more of transient form
> In her deep self, than some dead lake
>
> That holds the shadow of a lark
>> Hung in the shadow of a heaven?
>> Or has the shock, so harshly given,
> Confused me like the unhappy bark
>
> That strikes by night a craggy shelf,
>> And staggers blindly ere she sink?

And stunn'd me from my power to think
And all my knowledge of myself;

And made me that delirious man
Whose fancy fuses old and new,
And flashes into false and true,
And mingles all without a plan?

This poem has completely internalized the action and images of previous sections. "Calm" and "wild" describe only inner weather, and words rather than leaves have fallen. The opposed images of a calm, glassy sea and a ship in trouble recur here, but without any overt reference to Hallam. They seem at once the evidence of an obsessive regard for the ship and of an impulse to translate that obsession into self-regard. The oddity of this self-regard is that it works entirely through the medium of the poem itself. The poet does not remember his feelings, but rather reads them in the words of previous lyrics. The last ten lines, though clearly interested in the generality of emotional experience, express explicitly the concerns of a poet-mourner. The poet does not say that the shock of loss may have produced the mad alternation of "calm despair" and "wild unrest," but that it may have disabled him as a coherent recorder of his feelings, that those words may have fallen from him without due correspondence to his actual experience. The delirious man may or may not live a chaotic life. Certainly he writes a chaotic poem. Without knowledge of himself, he produces an account in indeterminate relation to his life.[6] Of course, self-knowledge is presently so tentative that the poet does not know if he is that delirious man or not. Section XVI, like section XV, proceeds by a branching that multiplies the possible accounts of experience.[7] A few lines before the confused and delirious man, the poet presents an image of perfectly determinate relationship, between the sky and the mirrored surface of the dead lake.

The interpretation of this difficult image leads into the central difficulties of the lyric. In his notes to the Eversley edition of his father's works, Hallam Tennyson offers one canonical version: the poet "questions himself about these alternations of 'calm despair' and 'wild unrest.' Do these changes only pass over the surface of the mind while in the depth still abides his unchanging sorrow? or has his reason been stunned by his grief?"[8] So the lake is an image of deep changelessness reflecting superficial change, while the unhappy bark, as Hallam Tennyson might have gone on to say, exists only on the surface. Its career is all surface and all change.

Combining this interpretation with the notion that the poem's concerns are specifically poetic might yield a revised paraphrase like the following: Do the changing poetic manifestations of grief signify inconstancy, or may words change while spirit remains the same? Or is the spirit wholly present in the wildly changeable surface? Such questions are obviously and variously relevant to *In Memoriam*, addressing the distinct and important issues of the poet's resistance to change and of the poem's adequacy as a record of experience. The unhappy poet does appear obliged to choose between an admission of change and a devaluation of the poem as an authentic expression of the deep self.

Yet the legitimacy of paraphrase is also at issue in this discussion of the relationship between poetic surface and depth. The images themselves must be worked through and not just translated into formulae. Here the true difficulty of the dead lake image appears. Both Hallam Tennyson's reading and the second stanza of the poem direct attention to the lake as an image of the relationship between transient superficial form and deep self. The image itself, however, emphasizes another aspect of the

> . . . dead lake
>
> > That holds the shadow of a lark
> > Hung in the shadow of a heaven.

This vividly presents the relationship not of surface and depth, but surface and sky. Furthermore, it does not portray the surface as the scene of constant and ready change, as the second stanza seems to predict, but rather emphasizes the static quality of the image. The surface of the lake is not a film, but a photograph.

By making the image of constant sorrow a dead lake whose surface freezes motion, the poet renders an instinctive judgment on the fealty to sorrow that he has sworn. The image also broadens the poet's critique of the lyrics that he has written. Vivid though they be, they fail not only the deep self, but the temporality of experience. Each lyric preserves the configuration of a single moment, or perhaps of a few moments, but cannot reproduce the movement of experience. Only the juxtaposition of lyrics does this and then only in abrupt transitions that force the disequilibrium of the unhappy bark.

Section XVI itself is appropriately discontinuous. The unhappy bark does not float on the dead lake of sorrow, but inhabits a new figurative universe. Nor does it describe a clear alternative response to a clearly asked question, but instead extends and complicates the inquiry already underway in the image of the lake. The staggering ship has no deep self and is about to sink into depths wholly external. The self-alienated delirious man has at least some other part from which he is estranged, but he, too, suffers from the confusion of movement. Each of these images exerts its own will and carries interpretation of the lyric in a different direction. This revolt of images from fixed meaning would seem to support the image of the poet as a delirious man, proceeding wildly from one fancy to the next, or as an unhappy bark, existing entirely on the surface without a deep meaning to organize and control the array of images.

Yet at the same time something abides and asserts itself repeatedly, as in the repetition of images from one lyric to the next, or even the repetition of words from one line to the next. Sorrow may be a changeling, but it has hardly changed to joy, and the poet strikes again and again the same deep notes. Martin Dodsworth discusses section XVI briefly in his excellent essay on Tennyson's repetitions, and remarks of its doubled image of the shadow, "Repetition is the mark of an inability to progress from one state of feeling to another, and arises from a sense of inadequacy to express the strength of feeling experienced . . . Tennyson's repetition is nearly always tied in this way to strong emotion; it is of the Words-worthian kind."[9] Not just an obsessive grief holds together the images of section XVI, but an obsessive examination of the relationship between grief and the words and images that strive to express it. Section XV opposed to the notion of constancy an image of change that was tentatively purposeful and progressive. In section XVI all motion is chaos unless linked to a changeless deep self of which it is the uncertain manifestation. Yet this deep self inhabits an ominously dead lake. Clearly the poet has not yet discovered what the appropriate work of his poem or his grief is.

The difficulty of sections XV and XVI indicates the bewildering variety of forces with which the poet seeks to come to terms. He examines at once the nature of his own experience, of the grief that he struggles to embrace and to conquer, of the change that he fears and desires; and he examines the problem of representing that experience in all its complexity. Nor can the two problems be surely distinguished, because grief both challenges and alters the powers of expression, and because both grief and expression must take place in time. In section XVI, the poet begins to deal not just with the lyric intensities of the moment, but with the extension of experience through time, and also with the extension of *In Memoriam* through time, its accretion of lyric moments. The poet still does not know if meaning, both in poetry and in life, unfolds through change and time or is defeated by them.

In the first movement of *In Memoriam*, the poet offers up his lyrics in resistance to the flow of time, each moment denying its membership in an historical sequence that threatens every human thing. But it gradually becomes clear that this is a *movement* of feeling, in spite of itself, and that the living intensity of the poet's feeling cannot help living in time. Of course, the poet can either welcome or resist this recognition, and he does both many times in the course of *In Memoriam*, alternately looking to history for salvation and decrying or denying history in the despairing or ecstatic

40

extremity of the moment. But individual moments and lyrics are always surrounded and placed by the mere history that they would master: the often discussed vision of section XCV being the central and unavoidable instance of such a placing—"frame" is Tennyson's word for it there—of unplaceable experience. The relationship of the rebellious part to the whole takes many forms in *In Memoriam*—the relationship of the part to the whole *is* the form of *In Memoriam*—and it is in the particular language of its parts, of one or another selection of memorable lyrics, that we can chart the poet's resistance to the leveling comforts of history and community, and to the suspicious comfort of the whole poem itself in its large movement out of grief. "It's too hopeful, this poem," said Tennyson, "more than I am myself." But Tennyson really did make that movement—as most mourners would—out of his splendid and isolated grieving and back into the ordinary and social progress of life. And he recapitulates this movement in the gradual and wayward progress of his poem, with its increasingly explicit awareness that it is a public and historical document.

Language, of course, is the public and historical medium of the poem, and section XVI, although it is the first lyric in which *In Memoriam* begins to interpret itself, is not the first in which it examines its own resources and the status of poetic language in general.[10] The question of poetic representation, though without the intrusive complexities of time, has already been asked, and more explicitly, in section V. Like other early lyrics, section V describes the poet's circumstances in the present, but it contributes as well to the important discussion of loyalty to Hallam and grief, and it alters crucially the ordinary formulae for the disparagement of language. The painful discrepancy between expressive need and expressive resources has been Tennyson's subject before—"I would that my tongue could utter / The thoughts that arise in me"—and will be his subject again in later sections of *In Memoriam*. But the poet in this lyric passes beyond simple complaint or regret to strike a bargain with his own language and with the public world to which language imperfectly connects him. Adequate expression is not a

41

personal craving only, not just a means of release, but a form of obligation to Hallam, to grief itself, and to the community that must know just what it is getting:

> I sometimes hold it half a sin
> To put in words the grief I feel;
> For words, like Nature, half reveal
> And half conceal the Soul within.
>
> But, for the unquiet heart and brain,
> A use in measured language lies;
> The sad mechanic exercise,
> Like dull narcotics, numbing pain.
>
> In words, like weeds, I'll wrap me o'er,
> Like coarsest clothes against the cold:
> But that large grief which these enfold
> Is given in outline and no more.

Not yet troubled by his own susceptibility to change, the poet does not yet doubt that a unitary grief underlies his expression. The half-sinfulness of expression arises rather from the peculiar powers and limitations of a language that both conceals and reveals. Calling upon Nature and clothing as models or analogues for this doubleness, the poet evokes Carlyle's *Sartor Resartus*, which appeared in *Fraser's Magazine* beginning in November of 1833 and which section V recalls both in its phrasing and in its emphasis upon the resources as well as the limitations of linguistic doubleness. In the clothes-philosophy of Carlyle's Professor Teufelsdrockh, visible Nature is the clothing of God, Nature and clothing both are symbols, and "in a Symbol there is concealment and yet revelation." But this is not to be regretted: "here therefore, by Silence and by Speech acting together, comes a double significance. And if both the Speech be itself high, and the Silence fit and noble, how expressive will their union be! Thus in many a painted Device, or simple Seal-emblem, the commonest Truth stands out to us proclaimed with quite new emphasis."[11]

The combination of high speech and fit silence might describe the lapidary language of *In Memoriam* at its best, but the poet himself claims less for his words and in stanza two confesses the selfish needs that are met by poetic expression. The rougher rhythms of line five suggest the inquietude that measured language, the perfectly regular iambs of the lines around it, can assuage. The poet is true to himself rather than to his grief in writing a language that numbs rather than expresses pain. In stanza three, language offers protection from the world as well as inward comfort, but it is a crude instrument either way, like dull narcotics or coarse clothes.

Considering once again the relationship of his language to the world, the poet employs a clothing image that seems at first a return to a naive conception of language as ornament, of words and meanings as separable and distinct. But this is also a new way to talk about the effective workings of his own language, and the reference to widow's weeds revises significantly the earlier model of expression by adding to it the notion of a shared human convention. Widow's weeds express only the outline of grief, because they do nothing to distinguish the uniqueness of individual experience. But they are eloquent in their muteness just because they are the conventional social sign of bereavement. Like Carlyle's devices and seal-emblems, they represent their common truth allegorically. Carlyle's symbols "have both an extrinsic and intrinsic value; oftenest the former only."[12] The arbitrary character of these signs qualifies, but need not lessen, their force.

Section V, it is true, lays stress on the inadequacies of language, but to complain that language fails is to employ one of the most common and most potent conventions of grief. For the poet of section V, elegiac conventions are the equivalent of widow's weeds, a generic signal of the generic experience of grief. This is one way forward from the impasse of the first stanza. To stress the simultaneous concealment and revelation that characterize language is to acknowledge, but also to accept, the mediacy of language, its distance from the raw materials of feeling. To accept and make use of the conventionality of language is to acknowledge another form of mediation, that of prior texts and of other speakers. The speaker who draws on an earlier and a common language purchases the certainty of some common ground at the cost of his original and unique experience. He enters a community.

Of course, every poet and every speaker enters such a community, and this is partly Tennyson's point, the point made by the casting of his poet as everyman. We hold in common the sense that only a small part of ourselves and our experience can be shared. But the point is more particularly applicable to Tennyson. Section V refers us not just to the conventionality on which all uses of language depend, but to the special blending in the style of *In Memoriam* of the language of other poets, and of Tennyson's own language with itself. Tennyson's allusiveness has been a leading subject since the Victorian critic John Churton Collins first delighted in catching the poet in the act. Recent critics have taken up the subject with more appreciation and less triumph: Robert Pattison, in his book *Tennyson and Tradition*; and Christopher Ricks, who has followed the workings of many of Tennyson's allusions, including even his allusions to the work of Arthur Hallam. Ricks has written especially well about a related and distinctive habit of Tennyson's, his tendency, especially pronounced in *In Memoriam*, to borrow words and phrases and key images from himself.[13] *In Memoriam* thus evokes a community of previous poets and, at the same time, becomes its own community of lyrics, a community within which repeated words and phrases and images acquire the status of convention.

Tennyson's poetry is conventional and communal in another sense. Even when his language is difficult, as it often is in *In Memoriam*—A. C. Bradley's *Commentary* gives evidence of the labor required to paraphrase many of its sections—casual readers seem not to notice the difficulty and to carry at least something away of the predominant feeling. Tennyson's language in *In Memoriam* is not conversational, yet it blends with its own distinctive extravagances of phrasing the short and pungent phrases of any person's speech and the common coin of other poets' speech: and these are all a part of the Tennysonian style that defined the voice of poetry itself for an entire generation.

The overt discussion of linguistic inadequacy, begun in section V, is continued in numerous later sections of *In Memoriam*, as in these stanzas from section XIX:

> The Wye is hush'd nor moved along,
>   And hush'd my deepest grief of all,
>   When fill'd with tears that cannot fall,
> I brim with sorrow drowning song.
>
> The tide flows down, the wave again
>   Is vocal in its wooded walls;
>   My deeper anguish also falls,
> And I can speak a little then.

After this, section XX begins with reference to "The lesser griefs that may be said," making the point clearly that speech is inimical to deep feeling. The climax of this discussion, as of so much else in *In Memoriam*, occurs in section XCV, where "Matter-moulded forms of speech" are indicted for their failure to capture transcendent experience. The poet has undergone a revolution of feeling, but language cannot reach either the heights or the depths.

But section V also begins, more subtly, a discussion of linguistic adequacy. Warning us that his words cannot tell everything, the poet moves ahead anyway, and in so doing suggests one way to think about the unmissable power and presence of the language of his poem. Each measured word is a confession of his fall into time and need and language, but also a stay against the disorder of history and the breakup of the self. The use of measured language is not just that it numbs pain, as the poet confessed in section V, but that it enforces discipline and takes the self outside itself into the shared space of convention. The therapeutic value of the poet's particular form of submission to time—and thus the aesthetic value of *In Memoriam*'s serial form—is that it forces each moment outside itself into a relationship with other moments that is not just consecutive but dialectical. The constant interruptions to our progress through the poem—the reversions of rhyme and the gaps between each stanza and each lyric—mimic the experience of consciousness as a series of new awakenings.

In Memoriam is an emotionally excessive poem, getting and spending its energy in the extremities of grief, despair, ecstatic assurance. But restraint can be another form of audacity in the Romantic tradition, and *In Memoriam* is also a poem about making do, about submitting to the flow of moments, to the uncertainties that succeed every certainty, to the gradual shift and change of feelings that will eventually become a large movement out of unhappiness, the cause as much as the consequence of whatever faith the poet holds. Making do with language means taking the language, like one's moods or the course of one's moments, as a thing given as well as created: "*Set* mechanic exercise" was the wording of section V, line 7 in the Lincoln manuscript.

Tennyson was a great public poet not merely because he wrote about politics, wars, the findings of the scientists—but because in recording the surge and flow of his own experience, he wrote the private lives of his audience. And he did this not by paradoxically exceeding the limits of the speakable, but by coming up against them and describing the experience. Section V succeeds by restraint and precision, by observing in each of its three stanzas a slightly different relationship of articulate language to inarticulate feeling. The poet's own feelings in the poem are neither underrepresented nor oversold. He protests neither too much nor too little the conditions of his entry into the public form of the poem, which are the conditions of his identity as a poet and of his presence to the community.

3

THE POET'S
EXEMPLARY
CAREER

Section VI attempts naturally enough to make some emotional use of the community invoked by section V, but the attempt is premature, and the thought that "loss is common to the race" provides little comfort to the poet in section VI and little power to a poetry that thrives still on the idiosyncrasy and privacy of emotional experience. The poet cannot yet abandon the desire to speak fully and for himself alone. It is later in the poem, after the first intensities of grief and after the dawning recognition that grief is itself a responsive and changeable condition, that the effort to give expression to his inward and wayward feelings draws the poet more and more into what he can recognize as the familiar and public forms of language. Reading himself, the poet is aware of being read. In the conventions of pastoral elegy and in the frankly historical thinking that enters the poem in its middle sections, he begins to assume overtly and self-consciously a special position in the community to which he addresses himself. The constraints and comforts of "measured language" are the constraints and comforts of the community, and as the poet begins to see his story unfold, the problem of adequate self-expression acquires a social context—it is the problem of coming into relationship with an audience.

The quality of this relationship, however, is determined not only by the poet's construction of his task, but by his success, by the quality of his language. It becomes necessary, entering the long middle section of the poem—from section XXI, through the lyrics of historical and metaphysical speculation, through the despair of sections L-LVI and to the climax of section XCV—to describe and to judge the different kinds and qualities of reading experience that its lyrics offer after the justly, if inadequately, celebrated intensities of the opening.

Relaxing his hold on the unique and uniquely experienced moment, the poet begins in these sections of the poem the poetically and psychologically constructive task of placing his experience in its communal and historical context and placing his moments in relationship to one another. But there are poetic and psychological risks as well. Besides the occasional local flatnesses of language, there is the tedium that can overtake a reader who does not match his own pace and pitch to the poet's halting and lower-keyed speculations. Besides the comforts of a discovered kinship in the unfolding history of the species, there is the poet's fear that he will lose himself in the undifferentiated expanse of history and community. Even as he begins to assume and to exploit his own representativeness, the poet offers repeated testimony to the idiosyncrasy and the privacy of his experience.

Although I agree with most readers that the greatest lyrics in *In Memoriam* are pockets of rebellious and unassimilated intensity, I want also to describe and to argue for the special value of Tennyson's public style, his gestures of affiliation and historical synthesis. The alternative to intensity through most of the poem is not tedium or flatness, but a sense of amplitude that the poet creates through the steady accumulation of lyric moments and that is the appropriate context for the analysis and placement of his own private and solitary grief.

Tennyson's earlier lyrics absorbed both the experiences of the conscious self and of the natural world into the mediate space of fictional and figurative language, and he seeks through much of *In Memoriam* the analogous achievement of a decorous and flexible style that is private and public at once, a style that will locate the poet centrally in the community he cannot help writing for. It is the language of the community, after all, and sections XXI-XXVII begin to draw out the implications of section V and of its acknowledgment that, although the poet cannot speak his soul fully in a common language, he can represent in such a language the experience of many souls and so join with them. Though not always at his best, Tennyson can write well as this sort of public poet—as a private consciousness in a speculative and existential mood.

The speculative mood opens onto history as well as onto community, and the poet's self-conscious willingness to be exemplary coincides with a new sense of his own career in time. Some pressure has been eased after the first twenty lyrics, and it is as if the poet, with so many moments behind him, has room at last to turn around. With his friend now buried and his own urgent grief beginning to take the shape of narrative, he engages for the first time in the historical thinking that dominates the middle sections of the poem and attempts to chart a course in time for himself and for his dead friend and all of their mortal race.

These myths of personal and racial history serve the poet in several ways and appear in several guises in the course of *In Memoriam*, importantly different from one another but with important features in common. We can preserve the crucial distinction between the Christian and the evolutionary models of human history, for instance, and still see both as the poet's way of placing his present and solitary unhappiness in the context of a familiar historical scheme. Locating his own experience in a larger narrative of development and fulfillment, the poet implicitly suggests a remedy and a rationale for his distress. If his own career has taken its pattern from the career of all mankind as given in the Old Testament, then he may draw his hope for the future from the redemptive promises of the New Testament. If the fall of man was truly fortunate, then so may his own loss yield ampler gain, and he can idealize the past without sacrificing his hope for the future. The reservations that he had expressed in section I about such an emotional and psychic economy are suppressed, surviving only as a kernel of doubt, the bad conscience of the poet's ameliorative visions.

49

But the resistance to history has other sources as well, especially when history is imagined not as a coherent narrative, but as the immensity that surrounds and dwarfs any individual life. The poet pits himself against history not only in the intensity of his grieving, but in his fear and joy as well, fear of annihilation and joy in the moments of ecstatic assurance that he is occasionally granted, those notorious later moments in which the heart is ready to stand up and answer "I have felt" (CXXIV) and to take its self-evident feelings as a sufficient guarantee of the cosmic order. In such moments history is either malign or unreal, and fulfillment is in the present or nowhere. Such moments repeatedly interrupt the poet's progress in *In Memoriam* to set themselves against the very idea of progress, and, frequently, their intensity and poetic power grant them a special authority. These moments, especially the moments of the poet's most sweeping despair, are what many readers remember best about *In Memoriam*, and, just as they stop the poet, they should stop interpretation in its totalizing course.

From the safe distance of speculation, the poet in the middle sections of the poem explores authentic anxieties about his daily conduct as a mourner, about the different kinds and qualities of faith, and about the relationships between life and afterlife, himself and his friend, the material and the spiritual, the present and the future. But his most sober and literal-minded meditations have attracted more scholarly attention and more critical condescension than they merit, and the unremarkable results of the poet's metaphysical curiosity are less interesting than its psychological conditions. One duty of the critic in reading these middle sections of the poem is to keep refocusing attention on Tennyson's properly poetic achievement, to identify as nearly as possible what it is that legitimately continues to draw readers—that ought to draw more readers—to the poem.

Tennyson's opinions about the nature of personal relationships in the afterlife can have little force for us, no more than those of any other anxious and ignorant mortal. But his need to believe one thing or another, and the circumstances of his ability to simulate belief, push us into valuable questioning and provide a compelling image of human thought and need in living motion. How does the intense grief of the opening trick and soothe itself into the apparently less threatening explorations of these middle sections? And what, if anything, triggers the violent interruptions to this exploration, the sudden collapse of the unargued confidence on which such exploration must depend: that things are somehow all right, that conduct matters in the emptiness of cosmos, that there are a spirit and a future worth naming? The poet's grief for his friend, when it surfaces in these sections of the poem, takes the form of a despair for himself that destroys all sense of confidence or community and that takes no comfort from the mystification of surrounding moments or the kinship of surrounding and mortal men.

We cannot reckon adequately the achievement of *In Memoriam* without some sense of the internal and thematic drama of the poet's relationships to community and history, and for that reason I am less interested in Tennyson's anxiety of influence—in his cooperative or antagonistic relations to Keats or Shelley or Wordsworth—than in the back-and-forth drama of individuation and assimilation that describes his poet's and his own relationship to the imagined community of the poem and the relation of each lyric moment to the whole. I have discussed already and will discuss again the bearing of Shelley on individual lyrics. It would be tempting, introducing Shelley's *Adonais* as the text behind later sections of *In Memoriam*, to press further the analogy thus suggested between Hallam and Keats. Both, after all, were geniuses who died young, and Tennyson's struggle to come to honorable terms with Hallam's ghost is a provocative model of interpoetic relationship. But in discussing the relations between *In Memoriam* and the poems of Keats and Shelley, I doubt whether the contest of influence in individual lyrics matters as much as the brute fact of Tennyson's survival into adult life and a certain kind of celebrity. It is true that the large differences of temperament between Tennyson and the more glamorous romantics have often been overstated and that Tennyson's relations with the customs and beliefs of his day were more thoughtfully and honorably combative than his twentieth-century detractors have often supposed. But it is also true that Tennyson intended to occupy a position in his society to which neither Keats nor Shelley aspired and that *In Memoriam* first embodied this intention in all its ambivalence.

Tennyson's relationship to Wordsworth is also fascinating, and especially to *The Prelude*, published in the same year as *In Memoriam* and standing over and around it as, it seems to me, the one long poem of the last two centuries that is clearly greater than *In Memoriam*. But between *In Memoriam* and *The Prelude*, as between Tennyson and Keats and Shelley, the most obvious differences seem also to be the most important. Is it not the shortness of *In Memoriam*'s lyrics and even of its lines that first and most clearly breaks up the poem and keeps it from the unembarrassed sublimity of Wordsworth's Miltonic strain? It is true that *In Memoriam* cannot be judged or even described apart from the world of poets and readers on whose existence it so self-consciously depends. But I am interested first in the complex description that attempts to spell out the implications of its internal and intentional relationships to the communities that Tennyson knowingly invoked and relied upon. Tennyson was a brilliantly original stylist, but it is less the stylistic particulars of one or another lyric than the genuine and productive ambivalence of this internal relationship to community that distinguishes *In Memoriam* from any of its imaginable lyric or Romantic sources. The tension between the singular and incommunicable intensities of experience and the creation of an exemplary narrative that assimilates them, between the moment and history, between the part and the whole, is still and again the focus.

In section XXI the poet imagines and gives voice to his audience in a self-conscious effort to locate his poem in a larger world of discourse. Worrying aloud about the possible misconstruction of his poem, he stops to answer the charges of emotional self-indulgence brought by an imaginary trio of readers—and later echoed by Edward FitzGerald.[1]

I sing to him that rests below,
    And, since the grasses round me wave,
    I take the grasses of the grave,
And make them pipes whereon to blow.

The traveller hears me now and then,
    And sometimes harshly will he speak:
    'This fellow would make weakness weak,
And melt the waxen hearts of men.'

Another answers, 'Let him be,
    He loves to make parade of pain,
    That with his piping he may gain
The praise that comes to constancy.'

A third is wroth: 'Is this an hour
    For private sorrow's barren song,
    When more and more the people throng
The chairs and thrones of civil power?

'A time to sicken and to swoon,
    When Science reaches forth her arms
    To feel from world to world, and charms
Her secret from the latest moon?'

Behold, ye speak an idle thing:
    Ye never knew the sacred dust:
    I do but sing because I must,
And pipe but as the linnets sing:

And one is glad; her note is gay,
    For now her little ones have ranged;
    And one is sad; her note is changed,
Because her brood is stol'n away.

    In spite of his resolution not to seek the "far-off interest of tears," the poet of section XXI begins in his opening image to play upon his grief, to make out of it the wide-ranging consideration of mortal circumstances that *In Memoriam* notoriously became. But this is at most a transformation, and not a rejection, of private experience, and it will require, where it succeeds, the complementary translation of public issues into the language of private and immediate experience. Science reaching forth its arms in stanza five is not the bold alternative to sickening and swooning, but another bereft lover, another of the images of mute, blind, groping need that haunt the poem. The mourner's voice breaks through here and he announces the force of his compulsion more effectively in this image than in the strained and self-delighting intensity of the initiate's reference to the "sacred dust."

The poet continues in section XXI to emphasize the singular and the arbitrary qualities of his experience, rejecting any broad, social construction of his task and rejecting, too, the notion that individual lives compose a rational pattern. The clipped phrases of the last stanza cling insistently to the simple, discrete facts of experience. Some people are happy, some are sad. No generalizations follow. But the poet does look to his audience in section XXI and, while insisting that he can write no other poem, he acknowledges that there are other poems to write, other visions of the world than his own. And section XXI also makes more explicit use of the pastoral convention than have earlier lyrics, even in claiming that it seeks no public hearing. What is more, the poet-shepherd of the first stanza alters plain fact to fit his pastoral figure. Hallam's body was not in the churchyard at Clevedon, but entombed inside the church.[2] Private experience can hardly help its translation into the forms of shared convention. "Private sorrow" may remain the poet's subject, but the private subject begins here to discover and to evoke its social context.

In section XXII the poet expands his gaze in time as well as in the world. Looking before and after down the path of life that is the organizing image of the next five sections, he resorts to a generalized pastoral landscape that might represent his own life, or anyone's. Like the stepping-stones of section I, and unlike the vividly and immediately experienced objects and landscapes of most other early sections, this path of life is carefully and accessibly typical.

> The path by which we twain did go,
>   Which led by tracts that pleased us well,
>   Thro' four sweet years arose and fell,
> From flower to flower, from snow to snow:
>
> And we with singing cheer'd the way,
>   And, crown'd with all the season lent,
>   From April on to April went,
> And glad at heart from May to May:
>
> But where the path we walk'd began
>   To slant the fifth autumnal slope,
>   As we descended following Hope,
> There sat the Shadow fear'd of man;
>
> Who broke our fair companionship,
>   And spred his mantle dark and cold,
>   And wrapt thee formless in the fold,
> And dull'd the murmur on thy lip,
>
> And bore thee where I could not see
>   Nor follow, tho' I walk in haste,
>   And think, that somewhere in the waste
> The Shadow sits and waits for me.

Once again, however, something has been lost, and the slackness and the sweetness of the first two stanzas are explained only partly by their function. The poet lapses here into the conventional imagery that will permit him to present his own past as the golden dawn of all mankind. "Flower to flower," "snow to snow," "April on to April," and "May to May" are formulae that describe an Edenic time without change or diminution. Only the fact of death, the presence of the Shadow, reveals that these perfect natural repetitions have occurred in the course of an all-too-linear human life.

In such a passage from one time into another, the poet reenacts the expulsion from Paradise into the history that he can no longer deny, and this opening into history thus coincides with the taking on of an exemplary role.

But we must distinguish the exemplary from the commonplace and the poet's ambitions from his achievements. The verbal deadness of his idealized past is a real and not a strategic failure, and it is representative. Tennyson fails throughout *In Memoriam* to write with any particularity or force about the actual circumstances of his life with Hallam, or, indeed, about the actual and quotidian circumstances of any social or domestic life. This failure is essential to the special character of the poem. Individual lyrics give always the sense—doubtless accurate—of having been written in retirement, away from the day's activities. Writing so exclusively and intensely from the moment, the poet cannot then carry alive into his verse any but the events of his consciousness as he writes, and the details of the day or of his remembered life with Hallam are as distant and hypothetical as the details of the life that Hallam might have lived on earth or that he enjoys now in Heaven. Tennyson writes about all these subjects, but never at his best, and he can rarely find for them a level of diction that will save him from obtrusively poetical effects. He can still be speculative—the mind can range widely even in a moment—and experience does not have to be intense or claustrophobic in order to be immediate. But it had better be immediate if it is to be poetically interesting, and what Tennyson and his poet feel immediately is more often a solitary than a social event, more often a present emptiness than a remembered fullness, more often even a present fullness than any merely remembered or reconstructed event.

I am not denying the power or centrality of Tennyson's celebrated "passion of the past," but only trying to describe more precisely the ways in which that passion is registered in his poems. Even so notoriously backward-looking a poem as "Tears, Idle Tears" scrupulously holds itself to the moment that the poet looks back from. Present consciousness is the real and exclusive theater

of the poem, and the beautifully expressive similes that are pro-
jected in that theater are not remembered images but images of
memory. Tennyson writes about the past as a felt impingement
upon the present and not as another scene to which the reader and
the poet can imaginatively remove themselves. His natural subject
is the experience and not the content of memory. It is when he tries
to write about how things were or might have been, rather than
about what he feels and thinks now, that Tennyson's language be-
comes abstract and second-hand.

Compare, for instance, the last two stanzas of section XXII, above,
with the dull sweetness of the first two. When the Shadow appears
to "spread his mantle dark and cold" and to gather Hallam "form-
less in the fold," we are back on Tennyson's proper ground and he
writes an accomplished and moodily appropriate stanza. Hallam's
death was a past event, too, of course, and Tennyson recovers it
only as a typical and metaphorical event. But this lack of particu-
larity is hardly as damaging here, in the account of an event that is
conceived precisely as the swallowing up of particularity, as it was
to an account of social and historical life. Better still, however, and
more characteristic of what *In Memoriam* does best is the last stanza,
in which the poet's deprivation assumes a particular and bodily
form. He might as easily have written in the present tense as the
past of the shadow that "bore thee where I could not see/Nor fol-
low," and then he does write in the present tense the best lines of
the lyric:

> And bore thee where I could not see
> Nor follow, tho' I walk in haste,
> And think, that somewhere in the waste
> The Shadow sits and waits for me.

Starting in haste and stopping to think, these lines live and move
with the living thoughts of the poet and place the shadow unspec-
tacularly in the real landscape of all of our lives.

In the lyrics that follow the poet continues the mythological ex-
pansion of his own history, imagining the past as the scene of mag-

ical repetition and reciprocity and the present as a lonely and faltering progress down a darkening path. But even as he adds important elements to his myth, his language veers often into a lifelessly abstract pastoralism.

> Now, sometimes in my sorrow shut,
>   Or breaking into song by fits,
>   Alone, alone, to where he sits,
> The Shadow cloak'd from head to foot,
>
> Who keeps the keys of all the creeds,
>   I wander, often falling lame,
>   And looking back to whence I came,
> Or on to where the pathway leads;
>
> And crying, How changed from where it ran
>   Thro' lands where not a leaf was dumb;
>   But all the lavish hills would hum
> The murmur of a happy Pan:
>
> When each by turns was guide to each,
>   And Fancy light from Fancy caught,
>   And Thought leapt out to wed with Thought
> Ere Thought could wed itself with Speech;
>
> And all we met was fair and good,
>   And all was good that Time could bring,
>   And all the secret of the Spring
> Moved in the chambers of the blood;
>
> And many an old philosophy
>   On Argive heights divinely sang,
>   And round us all the thicket rang
> To many a flute of Arcady.

The opening lines of this lyric follow closely the wandering and fitful movements of the poet to the central, cloaked figure of the shadow. But the landscape he looks back on is external and conventional, persuasively felt only when it enters the chambers of the blood. Compare the fourth stanza above with this complaint from section LXXXII:

> For this alone on Death I wreak
> The wrath that garners in my heart;
> He put our lives so far apart
> We cannot hear each other speak.

These are complementary statements, isolating a special comfort of relationship, first by celebrating its presence in the past, then by lamenting its absence in the present. Yet the evident superiority of the second statement to the first—its advantages of economy, force, truthfulness—are not merely the result of an unexamined preference for sadness over happiness.

The stanza from section XXIII does have its place in the argument of *In Memoriam*; it is not just ungovernable enthusiasm or an attempt to make things pretty for a Victorian audience, but an important addition to the poet's myth of his past. According to this myth, the present suffers a multiple division, from the past, from the antiphonal presence of the beloved, and the further division, now necessary, of inward experience from the outward forms of expression. Before the past fell into the present, experience had not fallen into the broken condition of language. In searching out a clear and effectual self-expression, the poet does not seek merely an outlet for grief, but seeks to recover the possibility of true human contact. With his dead friend he proved once that the self was not completely isolated, and if he could communicate now to the reader the full measure of his grief, the proof would be repeated. The present necessity of speech, however, makes such a repetition difficult at best. The poet relies on the archetypal character of his experience.

But with whom does the poet truly make contact in this image of leaping thoughts? Not with the reader and not with Hallam, the real gift of whose presence is far more successfully evoked by the straightforward lament "We cannot hear each other speak," a line that earns its first-person plural, and not just because of our melancholy suspicion that dead men can truly hear nothing. For once, the poet is not nervously apologetic about the asymmetry of his relationship with his dead and transfigured friend and he writes out of his immediate conviction that the loss of the bodily life is the loss of something precious. Quieter and less wrenching than "0 for the touch of a vanished hand / And the sound of a voice that is still," this line from *In Memoriam*, like those from "Break, break, break," draws its power from the sudden explicitness with which it names and mourns the simple miracle of physical presence. And it is suddenly, convincingly truer to the actual experience of friendship than the pastoral re-creations that deserve Dr. Johnson's strictures on "Lycidas" as "Lycidas" never did.

Neither the poet nor the critical reader can be satisfied for long with Arcadian reminiscence, and directly in section XXIV the poet stops himself to ask if mythology has not falsified history:

> And was the day of my delight
> As pure and perfect as I say?
> The very source and fount of Day
> Is dash'd with wandering isles of night.

> If all was good and fair we met,
> This earth had been the Paradise
> It never look'd to human eyes
> Since our first Sun arose and set.

The individual life cannot repeat the history of the species, because it is placed in history itself at a time long after the Fall. It was always in history and never in Paradise. Nonetheless, its own mingled origins do resemble "the very source and fount of Day." This is the sun, of course, and "wandering isles" are identified as sunspots by Tennyson's own note, but the image also anticipates the image of that divine power "Which makes the darkness and the light, / And dwells not in the light alone" (XCVI). The mingling of darkness and light yields in section XXVI to a vision of divine simultaneity.

> Still onward winds the dreary way;
>   I with it; for I long to prove
>   No lapse of moons can canker Love,
> Whatever fickle tongues may say.
>
> And if that eye which watches guilt
>   And goodness, and hath power to see
>   Within the green the moulder'd tree,
> And towers fall'n as soon as built—
>
> Oh, if indeed that eye foresee
>   Or see (in Him is no before) . . .

In place of a vision of history that distinguishes sharply between the perfect past and the fallen present, this poem suggests the existence of an ahistorical perspective that can see all the forms of change condensed into a single image. The poet returns to his insistence on a love that masters time, but now omits the once-obligatory deathlike clasp of grief. Instead the poet and his love stand beside, though he cannot yet assume, the divine perspective which can legitimize and aid the mastery of time. The grim denial of change that pervaded earlier sections becomes less grim and begins to see its way to a vision that does not vainly deny change so much as incorporate it into some larger apprehension of changelessness.

In section XXVII the poet achieves a tentative wisdom:

> 'Tis better to have loved and lost
> Than never to have loved at all.

Quoted by now into meaninglessness, these lines evidence an important new understanding. The end of experience is not the sum of experience or the only source of meaning. The poet has loved and he has lost, but the second of these has not canceled out the first. They stand side by side, and he holds both his love and his loss together, just as love and loss were both present in the past, even if loss appeared only to the God-like vision that can see "Within the green the moulder'd tree." This new temporal vision both complements and opposes the Christian myth of the fortunate fall: complements it by offering a God's-eye view of the linear history of man; opposes it by suggesting that man may strive to share this divine perspective now, rather than wait through history for the future event that will retrospectively redeem the present.

For it is the value of the present and, by implication, of earthly life altogether, that is called in question by the poet's long view. Whether he looks to the beyond in hope or in fear, the effect, either way, is to subordinate the present to the future, and this subordination is potentially damaging to his poetry. Tennyson's characteristic melancholy threatens occasionally to make of his poetry the dreamscape that F. R. Leavis has accused it of being, an anxious retreat from the intransigent and present world. But what happens in *In Memoriam* is far more interesting and self-aware than this, and we must step briefly out of our sequential account of the poem to see just how the value of the present is questioned, but also how it is vindicated and restored. In section XLV, for instance, a sketch of developmental psychology issues in an odd speculation.

> The baby new to earth and sky,
>   What time his tender palm is prest
>   Against the circle of the breast,
> Has never thought that 'this is I:'
>
> But as he grows he gathers much,
>   And learns the use of 'I,' and 'me,'
>   And finds 'I am not what I see,
> And other than the things I touch.'
>
> So rounds he to a separate mind
>   From whence clear memory may begin,

As thro' the frame that binds him in
His isolation grows defined.

This use may lie in blood and breath,
Which else were fruitless of their due,
Had man to learn himself anew
Beyond the second birth of Death.

The historical scheme of earlier sections is recapitulated here in general and psychological terms. Not just the bereaved poet, but every human being, must emerge from Eden into the world, from an innocence of self and time and language into the separation of personality. Tennyson has seemed to work in earlier poems, notably in "Supposed Confessions of a Second-Rate Sensitive Mind," from such a theory of identity, a theory that adequately explains the need in *In Memoriam* to rediscover the bases of community and has the incidental value of licensing the poet as a representative of his kind. The initiation of the self into time and language leads directly and inevitably to the fact of death, so that a record of intense and speculative mourning may reasonably grow into a consideration of the conditions of individual consciousness.

But the oddity of section XLV appears only in its last stanza, in the strikingly offhand suggestion that the discovery of identity may be the single purpose of earthly existence. Such a suggestion is more shocking than reassuring, because it so readily concedes that the meaning of blood and breath is in question. The far-off divine event toward which all things move at once confers value on the present and absorbs that value back into itself. If the anxious mortal looks forward to that divine event as the fruition and the redemption of all human history, then history itself is just a space between now and the end—"the secular abyss to come," in the phrase of section LXXVI. And each of our lives in the world merely prepares the way for a heavenly fulfillment such as the one that the poet imagines for himself in section CXVII:

> O days and hours, your work is this
> To hold me from my proper place,
> A little while from his embrace,
> For fuller gain of after bliss.

Here, as in other lyrics of anticipation, the poet reverses the conviction of section I and looks forward to find in loss a gain to match, and even to exceed, the pains of the present. But such anticipation may impoverish the present and leads also to the embarrassing humility of lyrics like section LX.

> He past; a soul of nobler tone:
> My spirit loved and loves him yet,
> Like some poor girl whose heart is set
> On one whose rank exceeds her own.

> He mixing with his proper sphere,
> She finds the baseness of her lot,
> Half jealous of she knows not what,
> And envying all that meet him there.

> The little village looks forlorn;
> She sighs amid her narrow days,
> Moving about the household ways,
> In that dark house where she was born.

> The foolish neighbours come and go,
> And tease her till the day draws by:
> And night she weeps, 'How vain am I!
> How should he love a thing so low?'

Subsequent sections manage to answer this last question and to recover the dignity of the poet, but he assumes the part here of a Mariana gone slightly silly. Enclosed in her house and her narrow days—a nicely odd phrase that works like the earlier line in which the poet was "sometimes in [his] sorrow shut"—the girl is any merely living person, and her reduced circumstances are those of all of our lives. The "dark house where she was born" recalls Tithonus, who looks back from Aurora's palace on "That dark world where I was born," a phrase by which he, too, means to refer to all the world on this side of death. But the phrasing here also recalls section VII of *In Memoriam*, in which the "dark house" before the poet is Hallam's and a real place, and in which the physical world is the scene of all the value that the poet can imagine.

Not that we must object to any intimations in the poem of a world beyond our own. I have no wish to dispose of so much of *In Memoriam*. But in section LX the poet can exalt Hallam and his "second state sublime" (LXI) only by diminishing the here and now. Our earthly lives might be revealed to us anew by a poem that could place them in relation to a larger world of the religious imagination. But the world beyond the world in section LX is only a sketch of the upper-class milieu that the poet already inhabits. The problem is not that the reader must imagine the poet as a girl or respect the assumed hierarchy of social classes—though these are problems that a successful poem would have to help its reader through—but that the poor girl's dilemma, and thus the poet's, is not freshly imagined in any but the third stanza. His representative interest and value are diminished in such a lyric in a way that Tennyson cannot have intended.

But Tennyson does not really value the world so little, nor is his poet so eager to leave it behind. Indeed, the poem remains obstinately attached to this life and refuses to imagine the surrender in any future existence of the particular satisfactions of personality, a refusal that provoked T. S. Eliot's charge against that poor thing, Tennyson's faith. Eliot complained of the poem that "the renewal craved for seems at best but a continuance, or a substitute for the joys of friendship upon earth," and of the poet that "his desire for immortality never is quite the desire for Eternal Life; his concern is for the loss of man rather than for the gain of God."[3] Section XLV, which seemed ready to sacrifice "blood and breath" to the uses of the afterlife, was also reasoning outward and forward from the experiences of the body, basing its faith on the survival of personality in the self-justifying vividness of physical life. And such a faith is absolutely necessary to the poet, as is made clear in section XLVII, which takes a position that nothing in the rest of the poem contradicts:

> That each, who seems a separate whole,
>> Should move his rounds, and fusing all
>> The skirts of self again, should fall
> Remerging in the general Soul,
>
> Is faith as vague as all unsweet:
>> Eternal form shall still divide
>> The eternal soul from all beside;
> And I shall know him when we meet:
>
> And we shall sit at endless feast,
>> Enjoying each the other's good:
>> What vaster dream can hit the mood
> Of Love on earth? He seeks at least
>
> Upon the last and sharpest height,
>> Before the spirits fade away,
>> Some landing-place, to clasp and say,
> 'Farewell! We lose ourselves in light.'

The poet knows what he must have, but he cannot see much beyond that first meeting or create his heaven out of any but earthly materials. In the abrupt and honestly uncertain question of the third stanza, the poet pushes hard on the vague faith of the Prologue, which looks forward to a future when "mind and soul, according well, / May make one music as before, / But vaster." Confessing now that he has no "vaster dream" of heaven, the poet confesses the obstinate limitations of his religious imagination and, in that word "dream," the mere wishfulness of line five's confident "shall." Without an answer to the question of the third stanza, he must imagine away the difficulties of eternity—the unthinkable boredom of endless feasting and vague enjoyment—in the escape clause of the end, which projects into the distant, heavenly future another death of another better-prepared self.

Tennyson's inability to imagine another life is responsible for the general weakness and the occasional absurdities of those lyrics in which the poet speculates upon Hallam's continuing performance of "those great offices that suit / The full-grown energies of heaven" (XL).[4] But it also brings the poem back again and again to its own strengths, to the accessible ground of the poet's present and living feelings. Fearing the loss of meaning through time, the poet must assert that time is the redemptive path to meaning and that we move toward some final satisfaction in the future, when "we close with all we loved, / And all we flow from soul in soul" (CXXXI). But he does not or cannot make much poetry of this unimaginable end, and *In Memoriam* is dominated instead by a recurrent and powerful resistance to such flowing visions of personality, and by a sustained attempt to claim the present and earthly moment as the scene of fullness and absolute value. Returning now to an earlier stage of the poet's progress, we can see the other ways in which this claim is challenged: by the ordinariness of mere, ongoing life and, most brutally and immediately, by the prospect of death. And we can see also and again how the claim is upheld by the insistent and immediate life of Tennyson's language.

In the earliest lyrics of the poem, value was identified with the immediacy and intensity of the poet's sorrow, and the claims of history and community were rejected on grounds of loyalty to Hallam and to feeling alike. As the progress of lyrics leads the present moment out of itself, however, the poet inevitably exposes himself not just to what is healing and hopeful in time, but to the fearful prospect of annihilation and to all the forms of loss from which emotional intensity was to protect him.

The waning of this intensity is at first a relief and an opportunity.

Conducted by his historical speculations to the resting-place of aphorism and to the confidence that, having loved and lost, he has not lost everything, the poet settles himself to a calmer accounting. Sections XXVIII-XXX are less inward than simply personal, an account of the family Christmas. Section XXVIII begins the fourth of the nine sections into which Tennyson divided *In Memoriam* in his letter to James Knowles. It is also the first of three "Christmas lyrics" in the poem and, according to still another of the organizational schemes that Tennyson proposed, the beginning of its second major section. The poet does seem to make a new and quieter beginning. He reports the extremities of his experience in moderate tones, and he opens his own mood to the authority of the world, listening to the church bells that ring out "Peace and goodwill, goodwill and peace, / Peace and goodwill, to all mankind" (11-12) and letting them rule his spirit. But the poet's troubles survive the season, even so, and the bells that "swell out and fail," "that now dilate, and now decrease," seem to foretell in their own rising and falling the wavelike motion of the poet's moods to come. For he still inhabits the closed room of his sorrow and even now hears the bells "as if a door / Were shut between me and the sound." The strained superficiality of the poet's will to recover is all there in the flatness of the lyric's final line:

> They bring me sorrow touch'd with joy,
> The merry merry bells of Yule.

When the moment is not full with the intensity of grief, it is empty of significance, measured against the hovering presences that are obstinately, painfully outside the poet's life. In section XXVIII, it is the ringing bells of everyone else's Christmas that call to the poet from without. In section XXX, his own domestic celebration is at first reduced to "vain pretence" by the "awful sense / Of one mute Shadow watching all," a shadow that is both Hallam and death itself. But something in the poet rises up in response to the occasion:

We paused: the winds were in the beech:
   We heard them sweep the winter land;
   And in a circle hand-in-hand
Sat silent, looking each at each.

Then echo-like our voices rang;
   We sung, tho' every eye was dim,
   A merry song we sang with him
Last year: impetuously we sang:

We ceased: a gentler feeling crept
   Upon us: surely rest is meet:
   'They rest,' we said, 'their sleep is sweet,'
And silence follow'd, and we wept.

Our voices took a higher range;
   Once more we sang: . . .

The lyric concludes in affirmation and the company recovers its tone, but I have quoted to suggest the effort and uncertainty with which this recovery gets underway. Although the poet and his family are able at last to celebrate the holiday, their heartiness begins in mere echo of the song they sang last year with the friend who has become a mere shadow. Once again "merry" is subversive, a word that shrinks rather than magnifies the positive emotion. And most striking here are the short, choked-out clauses with which the poet conveys all the labor and hesitancy of a song that may have started "impetuously," but that keeps dying out.

    For the reader, if not yet for the poet, it is the starts and stops and modulations of this voice that fill out the present and hold our attention upon it. While the poet strains toward some new security and community of feeling, toward a seasonally appropriate belief in Hallam's renewal and his own, the reader registers the fact of strain as it is lyrically reexperienced and values the here and now of the poet's language. Section XXX does not offer a report on any history off the page, but an engagement with yet another of the poet's tones, another chapter in the continuing history of his expression. No other persons come into focus, and the hymn that the company sings together is no familiar carol but an uplifting *In Memoriam* stanza, sung in the voice of the poet. But his failures as a domestic historian and dramatist of other lives need not be fatal to his poem so long as the line-by-line drama of his writing—how does he bring himself to say this thing, to hold this tone?—remains compelling.

In the lyrics that follow, the poet remains caught up in the reversals and qualifications of feeling that characterize his uncertain progress throughout *In Memoriam*. The constant play of thoughts and moods does not proceed always with any object in view. But there is always, looking outward or forward from the moment, the fact of death. When the poet cannot manage a merely nervous or urgent inquisitiveness about death, as in the lyrics on Lazarus (XXXI-XXXII), then he is susceptible to sudden confrontation with the unthinkable. If the significance of earthly life is diminished by the prospect of afterlife, it is destroyed by the prospect of a real and final annihilation. In section XXXIV the poet considers a possibility that he must hold at the arm's length of mere hypothesis.

> My own dim life should teach me this,
>   That life shall live for evermore,
>   Else earth is darkness at the core,
> And dust and ashes all that is;
>
> This round of green, this orb of flame,
>   Fantastic beauty; such as lurks
>   In some wild Poet, when he works
> Without a conscience or an aim.
>
> What then were God to such as I?
>   'Twere hardly worth my while to choose
>   Of things all mortal, or to use
> A little patience ere I die;
>
> 'Twere best at once to sink to peace,
>   Like birds the charming serpent draws,

> To drop head-foremost in the jaws
> Of vacant darkness and to cease.

The poet answers here the historical and emotional optimism of previous lyrics, and his life is apparently too dim to lend much force to the "should" of line one. If experience is to end only in death, then experience is without value, and a rough paraphrase of this lyric might be, " 'Tis no better to live and die than never to live at all." Stressing the roundness of earth and sun, of all creation, it insists on the meaningless circularity of a cycle that carries the conscious individual from an original to a terminal oblivion. The possible emptiness of the future drains away the significance of the present and, in section XXXV, even Love confesses its dependence on the denial of death.

To work without a conscience or an aim is to fall into the incoherence of the "delirious man" of section XVI and to surrender all possibility of meaning. Conscience and aim here are the moralized equivalents of origin and end, and a life without afterlife is thus mere "fantastic beauty," the object of an amoral aestheticism. Yet fantastic beauty is precisely the consolation that the poet offers the reader and himself in this lyric, as he brings forth out of dust and ashes the tropical vividness of the last stanza. The poet of section XXXIV is not wild; both his conscience and his aim dictate an appropriate sobriety. But between conscience and aim intervenes the earthly body of the poem, its richly particular and evocative language, and the near playfulness of that charming serpent is a refusal of deathly seriousness.

If the poet's own expressive energy will not quite let him think on his own death, neither will it leave alone his efforts at pious acceptance. Section XXXVI speaks out for the concreteness and simplicity of the Gospel story, and for the clarity of revealed religion over the vagueness of intuition. But the suggestions of its own language are at odds with its paraphrasable content:

> Tho' truths in manhood darkly join,
> Deep-seated in our mystic frame,

We yield all blessing to the name
Of Him that made them current coin;

For Wisdom dealt with mortal powers,
    Where truth in closest words shall fail,
    When truth embodied in a tale
Shall enter in at lowly doors.

And so the Word had breath, and wrought
    With human hands the creed of creeds
    In loveliness of perfect deeds,
More strong than all poetic thought;

Which he may read that binds the sheaf,
    Or builds the house, or digs the grave,
    And those wild eyes that watch the wave
In roarings round the coral reef.

It may now seem a peculiar definition of "poetic thought" that
excludes the Gospels, but I do not think that Tennyson is taking a
position here on the higher criticism, so much as contrasting the
public and historical evidence of the life of Christ with a tradition
of private spiritual testimony to which his own poetic thought is a
contribution. The first-person plural of the opening assumes a com-
munity, and the poet speaks, as he spoke in section XXXIII, for the
dignity of a religious position that he and a hazily defined group of
fellow liberals do not share.

The condensed and difficult first stanza, with its odd sequence
of metaphors, might serve as an illustration of the kind of "closest
words" and "poetic thought" to which the poet remains consciously
committed. Truths darkly joined are but darkly represented, and
we must reach for the poet's meaning into the neighborhood of
other texts: to the Bible itself for things seen "through a glass,
darkly"; or to section CXXIX where the poet's lost friend is "Loved
deeplier, darklier understood." A more significant example of poetic
thought, however—poetic thought of a more potently suggestive
kind—is the last stanza, which evokes an audience for the Bible in

language that suddenly removes the lyric into a new realm of feeling. This is a local instance of the general phenomenon that we have noticed throughout the poem, of the way in which the poet's own expressive momentum keeps leading him on into statements and sentiments that he has not planned or intended. Riding the changeable current of his own feeling, the poet does not know if he is lost at sea or headed home, and section XXXVI suggests a different answer to this question than it intends.

Alan Sinfield has written well about the unruly suggestiveness of the last stanza of section XXXVI, which conducts the reader first to the grave and then beyond to a sea "so overpowering that we cannot really feel very optimistic about the ability of the Scriptures to defeat it."[5] According to Tennyson's own note, the "wild eyes" of line fifteen refer to the island tribes who were just receiving the Gospels, but the phrase inevitably suggests something different from the mere absence of civilization. "Wild eyes" can hardly focus on a simple tale and seem to belong rather to the mystic frame of the first stanza or to the deliriously grieving mourner of earlier lyrics. No missionary's sail appears on the roaring sea, which Sinfield connects with "the homeless sea" of section XXXV, making the point that these associations are licensed and controlled by the context of the rest of *In Memoriam*.

"We have a vehicle whose tenor is completely absent," says Sinfield of this last stanza, and the result is a language that seems occasionally to assert its own autonomy—cut free from the poet's avowed conscience and aim—but that operates within a range of association controlled by Tennyson over the course of the poem. But this talk of linguistic autonomy calls up a set of wrong associations, too, and the issue here is not the separation of language from feeling, but of feeling from intention—the poet's intention, I would say, in section XXXVI, and not Tennyson's, which is well served. Reading *In Memoriam* sympathetically and adequately, we respond to the changing voice of the poet, its different moods and registers, as well as to the paraphrasable doctrine or recorded events that are brought to us by that voice and placed for us by its tones.

The most effective and also the most overt means by which the different sections of the poem are made to constitute for one another a field of relevant association is the repetition of significant words and phrases and narrative situations. A sizeable catalogue might be made of the forms of repetition in *In Memoriam*, the different devices by which Tennyson creates for us a world that changes and remains the same, a world in which the poet constantly absorbs and revalues his own recorded experience. Many readers have noted the way in which the *In Memoriam* stanza exploits rhyme as a form of repetition, the way in which each stanza seems to go away and then come home to itself in the fourth line.[6] Tennyson uses even the simple repetition of words within phrases, especially in the verbal formula "x to x," to give the sense of a whole life that "turns again home," in the words of "Crossing the Bar." There is the Edenic world of the poet's time with Hallam, a world that never left home: when the two friends are "glad at heart from May to May" (XXII), winter is not survived, but elided. There are the panoramic glances "from marge to marge" (used twice in XLVI) and from "coast to coast" (LXVII) that encircle the world in the identity, asserted otherwise in other lyrics, of East and West, Hesper and Phosphor, beginning and end. And there is the deadly undercurrent of the funereal phrases "dust to dust" and "ashes to ashes," which lurk behind so much of the poem, and are faintly touched upon in its own references to dust and ashes.

In the most highly organized and most obvious form of this repetition, word, phrases, and narrative situation are all repeated and two or more widely separated lyrics form an unmistakable pair or group. These groups include the Christmas lyrics, the observances of Hallam's death-day, and such pairs as sections VII and CXIX, both enacted before the doors of Hallam's London house, and sections II and XXXIX, both addressed to the yew tree. Section XXXIX was written in 1868 and then added to *In Memoriam* in 1870, and so calls special attention to the separate and creative act of placing the individual lyrics in the sequence of the finished poem. Revisiting the yew tree in the graveyard, this lyric repeats just enough of the phrasing of section II to establish a sameness of subject against which the differences in the poet's treatment and attitude can be measured. It seems at first that the yew tree itself is caught up in a process so powerful that the poet, too, must be remade. But at this early stage of the poem, the poet records a springtime transformation that frustrates expectancy and leaves all things the same.

> Old warder of these buried bones,
>> And answering now my random stroke
>> With fruitful cloud and living smoke,
> Dark yew, that graspest at the stones

> And dippest toward the dreamless head,
>> To thee too comes the golden hour
>> When flower is feeling after flower;
> But Sorrow—fixt upon the dead,

> And darkening the dark graves of men,—
>> What whisper'd from her lying lips?
>> Thy gloom is kindled at the tips,
> And passes into gloom again.

In section XXXIX, the repetitions of springtime offer only, in the phrase of the preceding lyric, "a doubtful gleam of solace." Echoing section III (in line ten) as well as section II, this lyric returns us to the poet's first grief as it is softened and brightened by the coming of spring. The echoes of earlier sections alert us to important differences, and Bradley notes the crucial change of feeling between "Thy fibres net the dreamless head" in section II and the near solicitude of line five above.[7] In the image of flower feeling after flower, the poet uses repetition to suggest reciprocity, both the collaborative fertility of nature and the human coming together of himself and his friend. But then comes Sorrow, "darkening the dark graves of men," and the final frustration of a gloom that passes only into gloom. This is repetition as grim sameness, the obstinate continuance of the present, rather than the restoration of the past. Section XXXIX condenses, in its final image a melancholy account of the poet's progress thus far, of the faint and failed beginnings of emotional recovery. But "gloom . . . into gloom" is a repetition within a repetition, and we can see, as the poet from within his lyric cannot, how much has changed between one gloom and another, between the sick and needy grieving of section II and the soft melancholy of XXXIX. And the reader knows, too, how much life and movement has intervened, how likely it is that a repeated gloom will lead on to a rekindling.

I have quoted already from several of the next ten lyrics in which the poet thinks himself forward and upward into the afterlife. "I have lost the links that bound / Thy changes," he says to his dead friend in section XLI, and he strives to reconnect himself to his friend and to the future in thinking through the progressive stages of life and afterlife. But he also approaches by these stepping-stones the abyss of sections L-LVI, for there is little sure support in the mere wishfulness of his accounts of the future. And there is more than a little bravado in the poet's claim in section XLI that "my nature rarely yields / To that vague fear implied in death." Even the confession that succeeds this claim covers up as much as it confesses:

> Yet oft when sundown skirts the moor
> An inner trouble I behold,
> A spectral doubt which makes me cold,
> That I shall be thy mate no more.

The poet of *In Memoriam* never quite says "I am afraid that I shall die into nothingness. I am afraid of my own death."[8] Instead, he puts one spectral doubt in front of another and the fear of death is mediated by community, translated into the fear of lost companionship or, later, of the death of the species. I cannot be certain, of course, that the fear of his own death was the original language of Tennyson's life-long insistence on personal immortality, and I contradict the poet's own testimony at some risk. But it is certainly to himself alone that the poet returns in his moments of sudden and irrepressible feeling. Straying too far into the relative comforts of speculation, as in sections XL-XLVII, he is drawn back inevitably to the inward landscape of his own deepest fears and feelings.

This return is motivated first by the poet's concern for sincerity, and sections XLVIII and XLIX are less fearful than apologetic about the fact that previous lyrics have stayed out of deep water. Returning to the imagery and issues of sections V and XVI, the poet says that he "holds it sin and shame to draw / The deepest measure from the chords" and that his lyrics, "short swallow-flights of song," have but skimmed the surface of his own feelings and of the deep religious and philosophical questions that they seem to answer. He has not proposed answers, he asserts, and does not claim to remove our doubts or to tell us what heaven will really be like, but has only let his thoughts and fancies go in the remission of sorrow's "harsher moods." Although the poet will speak his faith with more boldness and conviction in later sections, there is no reason to follow Christopher Ricks and Swinburne in questioning the good faith of his assertion in section XLVIII,[9] which places accurately the merely speculative faith of the lyrics that have come before. And in the lyrics that immediately follow, the poet does not retract this assertion but lives out its painful implications.

The last stanza of section XLIX, with its liquidly attractive sorrow, announces still a sense of security and constancy, and the poet reaps the emotional benefits of the claim that previous lyrics have been merely superficial. Given the anxiety of his earliest lyrics about the possibility of change, the poet cannot really regret the announcement here that his deep self remains untouched. Although his sorrow is genuine, it is both virtuous and voluptuous as well.

> Beneath all fancied hopes and fears
> Ay me, the sorrow deepens down,
> Whose muffled motions blindly drown
> The bases of my life in tears.

But superficiality has been a form of protection, too, and section L directly replaces this fountain of tears with a new and far less comfortable image of inwardness.

> Be near me when my light is low,
>   When the blood creeps, and the nerves prick
>   And tingle; and the heart is sick
> And all the wheels of Being slow.
>
> Be near me when the sensuous frame
>   Is rack'd with pangs that conquer trust;
>   And Time, a maniac scattering dust,
> And Life, a Fury slinging flame.
>
> Be near me when my faith is dry,
>   And men the flies of latter spring,
>   That lay their eggs, and sting and sing
> And weave their petty cells and die.
>
> Be near me when I fade away,
>   To point the term of human strife,
>   And on the low dark verge of life
> The twilight of eternal day.

"Be near me"; the poet calls out to Hallam, surely: perhaps also to God or even to the reader. Christopher Ricks observes that he reaches out to Shelley, too, borrowing much of the distinctive wording of the first stanza from *The Cenci* and *Queen Mab*.[10] He reaches, at any rate, for the comforts of community, against the sick and lonely fearfulness of a confrontation with meaninglessness and death. After the near pridefulness of sections XLVIII and XLIX, which suggested that the poet's true being was unreachably deep and self-contained, section L presents his isolation in a new and more painful mood. That it really is a question of mood is established by the order of the poet's concerns in this lyric, by the fact that his grim view of human existence begins in the unwilled mechanics of the inner self. The wheels of being do not slow in response to some observation of life, but rather condition the poet's way of observing. Time itself depends on the temporal indicator, "when," and there are times, apparently, when Time is a maniac, and times when it is not, depending on the poet's mood.

Connecting these times, or failing to, is the coherence or incoherence of the history of the poet's moods, of *In Memoriam*. Beside the image of Time scattering dust, we place the "delirious man" of section XVI, the "wild poet" of section XXXIV, perhaps the grief-drunk dancer of section I, and attempt to discover in the form of the poem a vision of order to put against its visions of decline and disorder and to tame the emotional violence of single moments. Beside the pained isolation of section L, we place the emotionally useful and strengthening self-enclosure of sections XLVIII and XLIX, the vision of merging selves that preceded and perhaps triggered it, and all the sequence of the poet's moods in the poem reacting against and following from one another in a meandering, but connected path. But we make these placements only by standing back and separating ourselves from the lyric moment, a movement in which the poet has schooled us by his penchant for self-quotation and self-conscious retrospection, and yet a movement that the poet also urges us to resist. Submitting to the authority of the poet's mood in the first stanza of section L, we move near enough and slow enough to defer until a second reading the different movement outward to the community of other lyrics, other texts.

Or at least until the second stanza. For even within the space of a single lyric, there is movement and change, a waxing and waning of intensity. The striking particularity of the first stanza holds us in its slow moment and compels us to share this mood that cannot go outside itself to consider another way of being. There is nothing in it comfortably familiar or nobly constant, and we are not drawn away to other echoed sections of *In Memoriam*, or, I should think, to the Shelleyan phrases that are here subsumed. But the mood has its own momentum, its own way out of itself, and the second stanza, as it begins, is immediately more literary and reflective, on its way to the therapeutic overstatement of lines seven to twelve. "Sensuous frame" is already a phrase that has to be reached for, that makes a point in its contrast to "mystic frame"—the seat of religious truth in section XXXVI (and in LXXVIII)—and that alerts us to the dangers of an abject materialism without at all convincing us that the poet's body was really racked with pangs. These are no longer reports from the front, but rather a series of brilliantly effective rhetorical gestures that lift the poet in the third stanza to the height of satiric overview. This is not satire, of course; the poet describes a terrible pessimism that he does not want to feel. But he describes it with a controlled virtuosity that bespeaks the satirist's separation from his object.

At the close, although the poet's light is still low, he knows at least what use he would make of his dead friend, and he looks forward to glimpse on his own the coming day that he would ask his friend to show him. "Fade away" returns us to the scary sickness of the opening, but the rest is a Tennysonianly lovely gloom—truly lovely, but somehow manageable. "Be near me when my light is low"; nothing says so explicitly in that first line, but we feel that the poet's light is low right now as he writes and as we read, and that the request for comfort and company is all that he can manage, all that keeps him from the complete despair of silence. By the end of the lyric he has talked his way forward once again to the greater health and openness of anticipation.

But if the opening request for Hallam's presence expresses a new and urgent need, it also suggests a new ambition, a newly conceived way of filling the present with all that the poet wants. Our own responsive nearness is a familiar form of intimacy and poetic success. We, at least, answer the poet's call and make with him a community of scared and insufficient mortals. The possibility that Hallam may answer, too, gives the poem a new goal and point of orientation. Against the models of history that reduce the significance of the present and the models of community that permit the poet to share only what is common in his experience, the poet has offered thus far only the intensity and particularity of his grief, with its denial of all else. What he seeks to lay hold of in the series of lyrics that lead up to and away from the climax of section XCV is a more enviable form of intensity and a sense of the moment as sufficient, but not blind.

Section L, however, is far from such a culmination, and it stands apart from any schemes of fulfillment, preparing more immediately for the recoil into ordinariness of sections LI-LII and then for the more resounding collapse of LIV. Section LI begins by echoing the language and concerns of L in a reassuringly calm series of questions:

> Do we indeed desire the dead
> Should still be near us at our side?
> Is there no baseness we would hide?
> No inner vileness that we dread?

Although the poet takes such questions seriously, he has answered them in the unworried affirmative in just a few lines, and their real function here is to aid in the recovery of his emotional balance, to put him one step further from the moment when he did indeed desire Hallam's nearness, and with an urgency that had no time for this decorous shame.

Section LIII performs a similar operation, asking a structurally crucial question in an unthreateningly mundane form. Thinking on the lives of men who have grown from wild youths into responsible fathers, the poet considers the implications of the doctrine that wild oats prepare a better crop, that present evil may be the condition of future good. He rejects the doctrine on moral grounds—it might be used to justify any bad behavior—but the hovering question is not simply a moral one. As he has done in a variety of moods and contexts since section I, the poet balances the costs and gains of a view of life that balances costs and gains and that looks to the future as a corrective of the present. This is a consideration of Providence as well as of prudence, of the hope that God himself takes charge of the balance. But section LIII is exceptional in its own prudence, and the poet cannot often choose his opinions so deliberately. More characteristic and far more disturbed and disturbing is section LIV, an account of the unwilled and oddly triggered impulses that compel the poet to believe or not to believe in the progressive order of things.

> O yet we trust that somehow good
>   Will be the final goal of ill,
>   To pangs of nature, sins of will,
> Defects of doubt, and taints of blood;
>
> That nothing walks with aimless feet;
>   That not one life shall be destroy'd,
>   Or cast as rubbish to the void,
> When God hath made the pile complete;
>
> That not a worm is cloven in vain;
>   That not a moth with vain desire
>   Is shrivell'd in a fruitless fire,
> Or but subserves another's gain.
>
> Behold, we know not anything;
>   I can but trust that good shall fall
>   At last—far off—at last, to all,
> And every winter change to spring.
>
> So runs my dream: but what am I?
>   An infant crying in the night:
>   An infant crying for the light:
> And with no language but a cry.

Looking outward from the trusting mood of the present, the poet attempts to comprehend those other moods that will be the undoing of this one and takes up the blood and pangs of section L—"pangs that conquer trust"—and takes up doubt itself into a larger and providential order. But with its opening "O yet," this lyric begins in reaction against what has come before, and its trust in the providential patterning of moments is but the function of a particular moment. Doubt and trust are side by side in time, neither one encompassing or cancelling the other.

Even in the present, the poet's trust is flawed and shaky. The vagueness of "somehow" in the first line is echoed in the "far off" of line fifteen, and both sound more mournful than trustful. Whether God's "pile" of lives is cast away or not, the image confers no dignify on any life in particular. The idea that one dead creature may subserve the gain of another is as unattractively mercantile as the calculated profits and losses of section I, and seems to lead on readily to the celebrated image in section LVI of "Nature, red in tooth and claw." So it is unsurprising that this project of trust should collapse of its own weight at line thirteen. Unable to sustain a mood that is so dangerously intimate with its opposite, the poet moves ahead into one of the tainted and doubtful moments that he has envisaged. He does not withdraw his trust in the future, but names it negatively—"Behold we know not anything; / I can but trust . . ."—and finds it inadequate. As so often in *In Memoriam*, the poet changes his mood, rather than his mind, and moves from one feeling to the next without altering the paraphrasable content of his world-view.

A faith in the redemptive power of the future is apparently a communal endeavor and this shift of moods is accompanied by the crucial shift of pronouns at line fourteen. The failure of common knowledge returns the poet to the individual act of faith, and the lines that follow emphasize the distance that separates the individual from the history he wishes to believe in and the community he wishes to join. Looking toward the future, the poet looks across an immense gap of time. Between "the far-off interest of tears" that the poet scorned to reach for in section I and the "one far-off divine event" that the Epilogue anticipates in all its solidity comes the faintness and longing of the far-off prospect of section LIV. "That good shall fall / At last—far off—at last to all" is more a threat than a promise until those last two words, and even they hardly keep the promise from dying away in our ears.

Trusting that every winter shall change to spring, the poet must trust, too, that his own grief and death are included and protected by this metaphor, that he is a part of something larger than himself.

But in his solitude, nothing can stop the erosion of trust, and the poet interrupts and undercuts himself into the sudden and infantile smoothness of the last three lines. Trust declines into dream and the strong "I" into an infant whose inarticulateness is the measure of his isolation. This is the infant of section XLV, who does not know time or language, and is now trapped by his unenviable ignorance in a night whose end he cannot foresee. Asking "What am I?" the poet strikes at the strong center of all his meditations, at the speaking self whose intense and articulate feelings have been his surest signs of life and thus the surest antidote to all his fears.

Going outside this moment to the consciousness that day follows night and that another lyric succeeds this one, we are conscious that the self who has no language but a cry is sponsored by the self who writes and who has produced, even at this nadir, the beautifully and appropriately infantile rhymes and repetitions—night crying out for light—of the last stanza. No moment in the poem is without this context, without our knowledge that one moment follows another and that a presentable and articulate self stands behind its language, just as we stand before it. Reading a single section of *In Memoriam*, we fall into its lyric space only to pass through it and emerge blinking on the other side. Our experience as readers thus matches that of the poet, for whom consciousness is a constant series of repetitions, enchantments, and reawakenings. Reading the last stanza of section LIV or the first of section L, we are held in place by an expressive power that also urges us outward and onward to consider the intention that guides this language, the meaning that it reaches for. Here, at the grim center of *In Memoriam*, we are characteristically given no single moment of greatest despair, but a pattern of related moments, a virtuosity and variety of despair. And this despair, like the charged and changing grief of earlier lyrics, is both the evidence and the cause of imaginative activity, an incitement to us to rechart the poet's course.

The light that was low in section L has gone out in section LIV, and the poet has moved backward from twilight into night and from the mature sufferings of one who sits up late to the cries of the nursery. But he is not without language for long and section LV recovers a handsomely speculative voice to ask how it is that Nature leads us away from our God-given intuitions of immortality:

> Are God and Nature then at strife,
> That Nature lends such evil dreams?
> So careful of the type she seems,
> So careless of the single life.

There must be a way around the implications of this long and wide view of nature, and the poet, "considering everywhere / Her secret meaning" is once again drawn out of himself. He is once again the representative man struggling down the path of life:

> I falter where I firmly trod,
> And falling with my weight of cares
> Upon the great world's altar-stairs
> That slope thro' darkness up to God,
>
> I stretch lame hands of faith, and grope,
> And gather dust and chaff, and call
> To what I feel is Lord of all,
> And faintly trust the larger hope.

But this bold speculation only returns the poet to the shaky ground of "what I feel," and his feelings are not secure and contained, but ordinarily dependent on what he sees in the world around him. It should not matter, if God and Nature are at strife, whether death overtakes the species or not. But the poet takes up this question even so, or is taken up by it, and reacts against his own words in the characteristic piece of self-quotation that begins section LVI:

> 'So careful of the type?' but no.
> From scarped cliff and quarried stone
> She cries, 'A thousand types are gone:
> I care for nothing, all shall go.'

In this new moment, the poet's own voice of a moment ago and the voice of nature are equally alien and equally matched. Pursuing the awful implications of a "Nature, red in tooth and claw," the poet rises out of himself and out of private despair to speak a vigorous denunciation on behalf of his species, but this mood, too, wears itself out and produces something new. At the end of his tirade the poet is suddenly private and fearful again, but weirdly calm.

> O life as futile, then, as frail!
> O for thy voice to soothe and bless!
> What hope of answer, or redress?
> Behind the veil, behind the veil.

The fourth line, with its quiet repetition, tries to soothe the spasms of feeling in the first three. Arriving finally at the dead end of nihilism, a prospect that he has merely glimpsed in such earlier lyrics as XXXIV, the exhausted poet moves through the moment, propelled by neither argument nor conviction, but by the saving motion of his own imagination. Both in and out of his poetry, Tennyson based his faith in a life after death chiefly on the monstrous unthinkability of the alternative. He simply would not believe that all things lead to nothing, and the life and force of his destructive imaginings seem calculated to produce in us and in himself the saving recoil, the irresistible urge to disbelieve our disbelief.

Sections LVI and LVII recapitulate this characteristic imaginative movement, the reaction of despair against itself and the taking up of despair into another larger narrative, larger, at least, from the vantage of the new moment. Section LVII returns to the grave and to sorrow, and treats the giant perspective of LVI as a mere interruption to the true business of grieving:

> Peace; come away: the song of woe
> Is after all an earthly song:
> Peace; come away: we do him wrong
> To sing so wildly: let us go.

Come; let us go: your cheeks are pale;
   But half my life I leave behind:
   Methinks my friend is richly shrined;
But I shall pass; my work will fail.

Yet in these ears, till hearing dies,
   One set slow bell will seem to toll
   The passing of the sweetest soul
That ever look'd with human eyes.

I hear it now, and o'er and o'er,
   Eternal greetings to the dead;
   And 'Ave, Ave, Ave,' said;
'Adieu, adieu' for evermore.

The short, clipped, repetitive phrases of the opening decisively turn the poet from the urgent questioning of section LVI, just as they turn the poet and his fellow mourners from the grave where they are suddenly standing, as if everything between this moment and the funeral of section XVIII has been a dream. The poet shakes off his wild fear—he will never feel it again in the poem—and returns yet again to the sorrow that is here a steadying influence. But even within this calm there is an inward dialogue, the "but" and "but" and "yet" of lines six, eight, and nine, marking the shifts and reactions. With "Your cheeks are pale" the poet addresses himself, dramatizing the way in which these lyrics permit him to stand beside himself, one mood counseling and correcting another. "But half my life I leave behind" may then be the explanation of the pallid self, and "I shall pass; my work will fail" the last, faint expression of his nihilistic despair. This voice is finally stilled by another that the poet hears and vows he will always hear, speaking the mournful repetitions of the last two lines.

"I hear it now"; with this announcement the poet claims the immediacy of lyric address and holds us with him in the time and place of his utterance. But where is he standing? Tennyson's own note identifies the rich shrine of line seven as the lyrics of *In Me-*

moriam, a metaphor that places the poet in this lyric not just at graveside, but at the edge of his own poem, overlooking the work just done and consigning it, too, to the dead past. But the real present of section LVII is placed and replaced in its turn by the opening of section LVIII, "In those sad words I took farewell," a line in which the poet steps outside himself once again, outside his own words, to comment on the beautiful sadness of LVII as one mood among many. Considering in this lyric the world "Of hearts that beat from day to day," the poet considers the gathering effect of his sad words, the effect on us of his poem thus far. The "high Muse" that speaks the conclusion to section LVIII, and encourages the poet to "Abide a little longer here," and to keep writing his poem, is another of the outside voices that the poet stations in his lyrics to represent the power not himself that draws him through the poem.

If the poet's works can die, as he has feared, it is only because they move and live, and their motion is in the direction of the community of readers and of the future that is an aesthetic as well as an experiential fact. The poem that can call itself incomplete, as *In Memoriam* does in section LVIII, acknowledges its own future, just as it acknowledged its past in earlier lyrics, and suggests, in Tennyson's words about "Ulysses," "the need of going forward." Going forward from section LVIII, the poet increasingly urges on us the habit of looking forward, and the success with which he orients us toward the future will depend on the success of future lyrics in matching the power of what has come before and making of themselves its necessary and organizing completion. But for now, in section LVIII, this pointing toward the future is rather a confirmation of open-endedness than of teleology. The next lyric is always there for the poet and for the reader, but merely as a drifting continuation or a new beginning, the potential outbreak of ungovernable feeling, and we are likelier to have been impressed thus far by the nearly autonomous changeableness of the poet's moods than by the purposeful coherence of their sequence. After a few dozen lyrics of relative emotional comfort and safety, sections L-LVI are suddenly both a vision and an evidence of decline, and sections LVII and LVIII moderate despair without at all redeeming it or restoring order. At one moment or another, the individual lyrics of *In Memoriam* have discovered the consolations of fancy or of forgetfulness or of their own imaginative life. Taking all of these moments, however, as a collected and interpretable history, poet and reader can take comfort only in the uncertain evidences of whatever power it is—and it might yet be God or history or the poet's own imagination—that carries each mood and moment forward out of itself and into an uncertain future.

4

MOMENTS
OF
VISION

When the voice out of darkness speaks in section
LVI—and this voice is no less mysterious for being the poet's own—
it is to quiet fears and to offer hope, "Behind the veil, behind the
veil." But where does this veil fall, and how can it be lifted to reveal
the truths beyond? It falls surely between life and death, and the
poet can go beyond it in one way by advancing through time to the
crossing of his own death, but this is a prospect that could cheer
and support only the already faithful. The image of the veil also
refers forward, however, to its other uses in the poem, notably to
sections LXVII and CIII. The veil in these lyrics does not await the
poet in the future, but signifies another sort of barrier to transcend-
ence, and may be brought in harmony with other of the poem's
tentative models of history. In the dream-vision of section CIII, a
veil covers the living statue of the reborn Hallam, and it is thus the
mystery of Hallam's death rather than his own that the poet must
penetrate in order to discover his reassurances. Closer at hand is
the quiet and more nearly natural vision of LXVII:

> When on my bed the moonlight falls,
>   I know that in thy place of rest
>   By that broad water of the west,
> There comes a glory on the walls:
>
> Thy marble bright in dark appears,
>   As slowly steals a silver flame

Along the letters of thy name,
And o'er the number of thy years.

The mystic glory swims away;
From off my bed the moonlight dies;
And closing eaves of wearied eyes
I sleep till dusk is dipt in gray:

And then I know the mist is drawn
A lucid veil from coast to coast,
And in the dark church like a ghost
Thy tablet glimmers to the dawn.

"That broad water of the west" is the Severn river, according to Tennyson's note, but it is the kind of phrase that Tennyson uses in *Idylls of the King* to render English places mythical. The poet comforts himself in this lyric by thinking that the same moonlight falls on his own bed as on the vault in which his friend is buried and by thinking that each is faintly lighted by the dawn. But he transforms these merely natural facts into "mystic glory" by the matched power of his vision and expression. Although he works only from what he "know[s]" (lines two and thirteen), and although it is only the moonlight on the marble tablet that he envisions, the quality of his attention renders this light miraculous and purposeful as it moves toward and across the letters of his dead friend's name.

In the lyrics that follow LXVII the poet considers in several different moods and situations the power of words and mental images to simulate the presence of his lost friend. It will be Hallam's own words in section XCV, as recorded in his letters, that precipitate the most urgently and convincingly felt sense of his presence that the poet is to have. In the figure of section LXVII, the tablet that bears Hallam's name is "like a ghost," brought partly to life by the poet's imagination and by the words it bears. It is only a ghost, of course, only *like* a ghost, but even a ghost is more alive than a stone. It must be the ghost of somebody, just as this piece of stone is now "Thy marble" and "Thy tablet," the extension and the remnant of a human presence. And this ghost at dawn glimmers on the verge of something.

The poet is calm and well in section LXVII, not because of his confidence in the future, but because he makes contact now, however ghostly, with his dead friend. The veil that covers the sky expands from coast to coast in space and not in time, and the poet's verbal repetition and his panoramic vision hold together East and West, the beginning and the end of things, in a vision of simultaneity. The veil here does not separate the living from the dead or the present from the future, but the phenomenal from the visionary, and it might be penetrated not just by taking the long march to the end of life, but by some visionary and still unimaginable ascent.

I have spoken already of the peculiar modesty of sections LX-LXV, in which the poet tries to suggest the infinite enlargement of his friend's spirit by stressing the meagerness of his own merely human estate. Although this modesty doubtless has its distinctive psychological sources and implications, it is, within the structure of the poem, a logical extension of "Behold we know not anything," from section LVI. In that lyric, the poet's ignorance was of the future, of what will happen "at last—far off—at last." Starting again from what he "knows" in section LXVII, he begins anew the search for reassurance, but in a new form and by a new route, a route that will lead him eventually to the trance of section XCV. This new form of knowing begins in the present and expands outward and upward, toward extraordinary states of consciousness, rather than forward in time. Although such a present consciousness may claim in its grandest moments to include the future, it does not bother to predict it.

The expansion of present knowing proceeds at first by querying the emotional and epistemological value of dreams and visions. The poet knows that such experiences are not reliable, but they are not conjectural either—they really happen to him, just as the peace of section LVII or the lovely and different peace of section LXVII really happens to him—and they provide a new evidence and experience that must be recorded. The poet has always had visions of a kind, has seen his friend again and again in the mind's eye, heard him and touched his hand with the mind's other senses. But he makes now a less painful and far more deliberate attempt to conjure up an image of his friend. These are not sudden and intrusive recollections, but pictures and stories with all the artful and interpretable shape that their connection with dreams suggests.

The poet's explorations of inner space are even preceded, in section LXVI, by a strange and ambiguous fancy that casts the poet as a blind man, thus making the Miltonic connection between blindness and inner sight.

> He plays with threads, he beats his chair
> For pastime, dreaming of the sky;
> His inner day can never die,
> His night of loss is always there.

The connection with Milton is unstressed, of course, and the unsteady tone does not echo Milton, but bridges the gap between the self-limitation of the preceding lyrics and the grandeur of lyrics to come. The rhythms of the first line above recall section I—"Ah sweeter to be drunk with loss, / To dance with death, to beat the ground"—but then the next two words convert that beating suddenly into something directionless and impotent. "Dreaming of the sky" is also hard to fix, both weak and grandly aspiring, but then the next two lines are clear and assertive, and their insistence on loss and gain together is an evidence of balance and self-knowledge rather than of uncertainty. The poet in this lyric hits upon a way of acknowledging his loss while claiming the compensatory value and integrity of his inner life. Nor does he need to feel any guilt for this compensation, because the light coexists with the darkness and does not replace it. Joining light and darkness together, the closing image of section LXVI joins itself with other images of simultaneity, like the image from section XXIV asserting that "The very source and fount of Day / Is dash'd with wandering isles of night." Darkness and light are not distinct phases of a linear history in these images and these lyrics, but parts of an inclusive present.

Trying to bring disparate times together and to bring his friend into the present by one means or another, the poet seeks out a variety of dreams or fancies in the sequence of lyrics that culminates in section LXXI, with a dream that makes "A night-long Present of the Past." But this dream is already in the past as the poet tells it, and he can only wish for "an opiate trebly strong" to remove him altogether from the sorrowful present. The poet has had other dreams, too, but they are troubled, as in section LXVIII, or obscure and groping, like the dream of section LXIX in which universal desolation—"I dream'd there would be Spring no more"—discovers only an uncertain hope—"The voice was not the voice of grief, / The words were hard to understand." But these are all forms of unconsciousness, enclosed in the parentheses of sleep. Most interesting and most significant is the vision of section LXX, with its ambiguous connections to the willed and ordinary world of consciousness:

> I cannot see the features right,
>   When on the gloom I strive to paint
>   The face I know; the hues are faint
> And mix with hollow masks of night;
>
> Cloud-towers by ghostly masons wrought,
>   A gulf that ever shuts and gapes,
>   A hand that points, and palled shapes
> In shadowy thoroughfares of thought;
>
> And crowds that stream from yawning doors,
>   And shoals of pucker'd faces drive;
>   Dark bulks that tumble half alive,
> And lazy lengths on boundless shores;
>
> Till all at once beyond the will
>   I hear a wizard music roll,
>   And thro' a lattice on the soul
> Looks thy fair face and makes it still.

In sections XC-XCV, the poet discovers and affirms that true vision comes "all at once" (XCV, 35)—the formula of simultaneity—and only to a spirit that is quieted, "at peace with all," and only when the memory is "like a cloudless air" (XCIV, 8, 11). Section LXX enacts a similar drama, receiving its vision "all at once," too, and only by pure grace. The poet once again works from what he already "know[s]," but something more than knowing is desired. He knows the face of his friend in the first stanza, but he wants to see it, too. Striving to paint an image on the darkness, he strives to make something outside himself to which he can then respond. In one draft of the Lincoln manuscript of *In Memoriam*, the first line reads, "I cannot get the features right," but Tennyson improves the line in revision, by suggesting the way in which the poet wants both to create and to receive the image of his friend. He can bring out of himself only what is there, however, and the strivings of the will produce the obscurely suggestive night horrors of the middle two stanzas, a catalogue of dark fears and frustrations. Only when these visions have exhausted the will does something suddenly arise from beyond it to look on the poet and still his soul.

It is not clear where this face looks out from or whether the other side of that "lattice on the soul" is beyond the self as well as beyond the will. Nor does it need to be clear, because the poet is not distinguishing here between inside and outside, illusion and substance. The crucial distinction is not between more and less real visions, but between more and less effective ones. What else, besides its emotional result, distinguishes the vision of LXX from the hypothetical experience of the first stanza of section XCII?

> If any vision should reveal
> Thy likeness, I might count it vain
> As but the canker of the brain;
> Yea, tho' it spake . . .

All the scary shapes of stanzas two and three of section LXX were cankers of the brain, we may suppose, but if we do not call the attractive likeness of the last stanza by the same name, it is not because we couldn't. It is because we follow the poet instead, and, though he might have counted in vain the vision of section LXX, he did not. Indeed, he might discount any vision. Section XCII does not lay down general rules by which individual visions are to be tested, but acknowledges the perpetual possibility of doubt. The readiness to be stilled and comforted by one vision or another comes as surely from "beyond the will" as does the vision itself.

The stillness of section LXX does not last long, however, and in section LXXII, a fine and bleak lyric on the anniversary of Hallam's death, the poet greets a "dim dawn" that is untransformed by the visions or dreams of the night lyrics that precede it. It is a day that cannot rise out of its grim past:

> Climb thy thick noon, disastrous day;
> Touch thy dull goal of joyless gray,
> And hide thy shame beneath the ground.

Here is another vivid moment that gathers together the present and the past, but the poet's mood has shifted strikingly from LXX and from the dream of LXXI. The dominant weather of this lyric is just as compelling an amalgam of self and world and comes as surely from beyond the will as any vision. But without any evidence that the poet's mood is mending or moving purposefully, this "beyond the will" may begin to seem a formula for hopelessness and passivity as much as for miraculous intervention. Awaiting his experience, rather than creating it, the poet is led to reflect in sections LXXIII-LXXVII on the uselesness of fame or of any attempt to make one's own future.

These lyrics about fame are particularly about poetic fame, about the fact of the poet's own productions in time, and they make a particular point about the poetry of *In Memoriam*. When the poet discovered in section LXX that he was to be the recipient and not the creator of his friend's image, his discovery was not just about the epistemology of visions, but about the character of his own writing. His gift is not for portraiture, but for lyric expression. His poem cannot represent his friend, but only his longing, and he makes this inability the theme of section LXXV.

> I leave thy praises unexpress'd
> In verse that brings myself relief,
> And by the measure of my grief
> I leave thy greatness to be guess'd;
>
> What practice howsoe'er expert
> In fitting aptest words to things,
> Or voice the richest-toned that sings,
> Hath power to give thee as thou wert?

The second stanza calls on the *topoi* of modesty and ineffability and might be part of any memorial poem, even of one that did much more than *In Memoriam* to paint a picture of its subject. But in the first, the poet describes simply and accurately one condition of his poem. Expressing what he knows, as in section LXX, the poet can express only himself, and he produces the troubled images by which we measure his grief and his anxiety. Nor did he paint for us the "fair face" that finally appeared to him in section LXX, but only, and from within, the sudden wonder that he felt. Pursuing a course that he has not set—at least this is the fiction of the poem and probably a fair description of Tennyson's experience as he sat down to write one lyric or another—the poet writes still from within the moment and from within his experience. He does observe himself in some lyrics, as if from without, but he does this only by reading other lyrics, and the self that reads is already a new self and is always in motion.

Sections LXXVI and LXXVII revive an old solution to the threatening problems of history and, taken together, make one more kind of claim for the sufficiency of the present. Like sections LXVII and LXX, these lyrics rediscover the good moment, which is now the moment of utterance. Taking as their subject the fate of the poet's lyrics in time, they bring home the discussion of vision and transcendence to the actual ground of the poet's activities. The trick of these lyrics is to include and exclude history at once, to see it all— as vast a landscape of emptiness as in the despairing section LVI— and then to call it irrelevant.

In section LXXVI we "take wings of fancy" and "wings of fore-sight" with the poet, in order to ascend to the place and time from which the vanity of all earthly striving is evident. Sitting in at its own funeral, this lyric gets paradoxically outside itself and addresses its own author—"And lo, thy deepest lays are dumb." But the real story is not in this imaginary trip to the heavens and to the future, which tells us nothing new, but in the poet's unemotional presen-tation. In the last line, he sees the oaks and yews of earth as "the ruin'd shells of hollow towers," a phrase that unites them in de-struction with the poet's own verses and that recalls the "hollow masks" and "cloud-towers" of the poet's making in section LXX. All earth's efforts are vain, even the yew tree comes and goes, and the once crucial distinction between nature's time and the poet's is swallowed up in space. But this emptiness, "the secular abyss" of human history, does not concern the poet from his lofty perch, and he is calm.

Section LXXVII, "What hope is here for modern rhyme," I have quoted and talked about in the Introduction. It is a more interesting poem than LXXVI and completes it by making a response to the vastness of the future. The poet looks ahead to the time when his work will be lost forever, and he concludes that it does not matter, because "To breathe my loss is more than fame, / To utter love more sweet than praise." Such an assertion cuts the creative mo-ment off from history and community both, as the poet takes defiant refuge in his limitations. He can project no image of his friend into time or the world, he sings only his feelings and only for himself, and he claims satisfaction. But the poet does not just utter love, and section LXXVII is not an exhalation of loss, but an odd and particular fancy. So we value it, at least, and, whatever the poet's experience as he writes, the author has made our experience relevant by re-creating the lyric as one section of many in a published poem. There is always the next lyric in *In Memoriam* to give the lie to any overinsistence on the independence and sufficiency of the present. Claiming his independence from the vast tracts of cosmic history, the poet ignores or slights the history that he actually lives from one moment or one year to the next. The poet has held fast to the moment in other lyrics, other parts of the poem, but the change from the stricken intensity of earlier moments to the mellow sufficiency of these can only be explained by following out the references of the individual moment to something outside itself.

The next lyric after LXXVII is another anniversary poem, the second Christmas lyric, and like section LXXII, it connects the moment of utterance with other moments by the conventions of the calendar. It may be true that the poet can create nothing to last forever and that he must live for the moment, but every moment has an afterlife, even so. Holidays and anniversaries revive their predecessors, and section LXXVIII recalls us to section XXX, with which it is carefully contrasted. This Christmas falls calmly and without any of the unstable extremities of hope or sadness that marked the first Christmas of mourning. Grief has changed its character, and A. C. Bradley finds this lyric the nearest thing to "a turning-point in the general feeling of *In Memoriam*."[1]

But the web of moments in *In Memoriam* is tightly woven, and section LXXVIII grows out of section LXXVII, as well as out of previous holiday lyrics. We notice, from XXX to LXXVIII, that the poet's grief has changed, and, from LXXVII to LXXVIII, that his way of noticing this change has changed. "A grief, then changed to something else"; the poet's description of his subject was apparently incidental in LXXVII, but it is suddenly crucial to LXXVIII: "O grief, can grief be changed to less?" The poet concludes that grief has not lessened or died, but only changed, and this insistence on constancy and change at once is itself a familiar gesture, repeated from sections XVI and XLIX and LIX. Past moments and past lyrics survive in this variety of ways in section LXXVIII, and this survival is a general phenomenon, but its value is still unclaimed and its significance is still unclear, just as it is unclear how the change of grief is to be explained or defined, welcomed or resisted.

The poet has penetrated no mysterious veils in his dreams or visions or ascents to the heavens and received no certain answer to the urgent questions of earlier lyrics. But he has confronted and made use of his containment within his own experience and within the uncertain and ignorant moment. From the nadir of "Behold we know not anything," he has returned with a kind of knowledge born of self-interrogation and of the fancied expansion of his moments. His dreams and visions and fancies have been a form of spiritual and imaginative exercise, both the cause and the effect of the large change in mood that he has noticed. Learning and forgetting and learning again the inevitability of change, the poet has begun to accept the advantage of his own movement through time and of the temporal thickness of every moment, the coming together in the present of memory and foreknowledge, echo and anticipation. The survival of the past need not be a mockery of the present.

The group of lyrics following section LXXVIII is less a group than most other of the subsections of *In Memoriam* and, although it contains three beautiful spring-time lyrics on which I will comment below, it also contains some of the least consequential and least successful writing in the poem. In sections LXXIX and LXXXIV and much of LXXXV, Tennyson's language goes flat and is both prosy and too poetical at once. The poet remembers with his brother the time "Ere childhood's flaxen ringlet turn'd / To black and brown on kindred brows" (LXXIX, line 15-16). And he imagines for Hallam the vaguely, but intensely, wonderful life they might have had together, a life in which "boys of thine / Had babbled 'Uncle' on my knee" (LXXXIV, lines 12-13), and from which Hallam would have left behind "great legacies of thought" (LXXXIV, line 35) of unspecified character.

But none of these lyrics is without some display of the poet's characteristic, and often striking, habits of mind and speech. He continues the mental conjuring that is one response to his friend's absence: "I make a picture in the brain; / I hear the sentence that he speaks" (LXXX, line 9-10). And he balances these simulations of presence with the recognition that no conjuring fancy can restore the past to its tangible and former life (LXXXII, lines 13-16):

> For this alone on Death I wreak
> The wrath that garners in my heart;
> He puts our lives so far apart
> We cannot hear each other speak.

In section LXXXI, the poet has credited death with filling the present in another way, by maturing all at once the love for Hallam that would have grown gradually if he had lived:

> This haunting whisper makes me faint,
> 'More years had made me love thee more.'
>
> But Death returns an answer sweet:
> 'My sudden frost was sudden gain,
> And gave all ripeness to the grain,
> It might have drawn from after-heat.'

This is a covert and a doubly significant admission: the poet concedes that he has profited from his friend's death and been forced by it into a love whose intensity would have surprised his innocent, earlier self; and Tennyson concedes—explains would be the better word if the significance is intentional—that his love is not the worldly and social love of friend for friend and that the intensity of his loss is disproportionate to any pleasure he had in the living exercise of friendship. Here is yet another way of registering the truth that *In Memoriam* is not effective or important as a record of Arthur Hallam or of Tennyson's feelings for him in life, but as a record of friendship lost, of what comes after the death of another. Section LXXXI acknowledges yet again that death has changed the poet absolutely and decisively, and yet this change is also a gathering and a compression of experience, the possible source of a strange and still unexplored potency.

Section LXXXV, the longest lyric in *In Memoriam* except for the Epilogue, attempts another kind of gathering, incorporating lines

and phrases from many earlier lyrics in a summary of the action
thus far and an attempt to answer the questions "whether trust in
things above / Be dimm'd of sorrow or sustain'd; / And whether love
for him have drain'd / My capabilities of love" (lines 9-12). In a
selection and reshuffling of lyrics for Palgraves's 1885 anthology of
his *Lyrical Poems*, Tennyson put LXXXV first, and it does speak in
the confident and oddly final tones of the Prologue. The poet an-
nounces that his friendship with Hallam "masters Time indeed, and
is / Eternal, separate from fears" (lines 65-66) and Hallam reports
from the beyond his vision of ahistorical serenity: " ' 'Tis hard for
thee to fathom this; / I triumph in conclusive bliss, / And that se-
rene result of all' " (lines 90-92).

The poem ends by offering a subdued friendship to some new
friend, probably Edmund Lushington, and it is partly, like section
LXXIX to Charles Tennyson, an apology to the living for Tennyson's
immoderate attachment to the dead. A self-consciously public and
accommodating poem, section LXXXV spends many of its lines in
constructing a bland and official mythology of the poet's recent ex-
periences. He claims that "My blood an even tenor kept" before
Hallam's death, and he is equally unconvincing in the modesty with
which he intends to flatter his friend's memory: "But I remained,
whose hopes were dim, / Whose life, whose thoughts were little
worth" (lines 29-30).

But there are moments as well of sudden honesty, movements of
authentic feeling, like this one that immediately follows on Hallam's
pronouncement of "conclusive bliss":

> So hold I commerce with the dead;
>   Or so methinks the dead would say;
>   Or so shall grief with symbols play
> And pining life be fancy-fed.

Section LXXXV also includes these puzzling and important lines
about the poet's "imaginative woe" (lines 53-56):

> Likewise the imaginative woe,
>   That loved to handle spiritual strife,
>   Diffused the shock thro' all my life,
> But in the present broke the blow.

The imagination is apparently a kind of emotional shock absorber, but there is also, in the word "loved," a hint of something unholy, a confession of the imaginative exploitation of grief that the poet has feared in earlier sections. Section LXXXV forges ahead to its own conclusion, attempting to leave behind such questions and reservations, but these reservations—they are matters of tone and statement both—triumph over the official version. In chastened and subdued tones, the poet announces himself ready to move forward into new friendship, but the past has not been set so surely in order, and the imagination continues its anarchic reworking of the poet's woe.

New beginnings are also announced in the three spring-time lyrics, sections LXXXIII, LXXXVI, and LXXXVIII, that are the finest of this movement of *In Memoriam*. The renewal of nature does not leave the poet's grief the same, as it so pointedly did in sections XXXVIII and XXXIX, but neither does it clearly turn him from grieving, and he receives from the season an ambiguous influence. Section LXXXVI is the least ambiguous and the most exquisitely composed of the three lyrics.

> Sweet after showers, ambrosial air,
>   That rollest from the gorgeous gloom
>   Of evening over brake and bloom
> And meadow, slowly breathing bare
>
> The round of space, and rapt below
>   Thro' all the dewy-tassell'd wood,
>   And shadowing down the horned flood
> In ripples, fan my brows and blow

103

> The fever from my cheek, and sigh
> The full new life that feeds thy breath
> Throughout my frame, till Doubt and Death,
> Ill brethren, let the fancy fly
>
> From belt to belt of crimson seas
> On leagues of odour streaming far,
> To where in yonder orient star
> A hundred spirits whisper 'Peace.'

Sustaining this single, long sentence is a mounting excitement so gentled and controlled that with the last word the poet seems to have received the blessing that he asks for. The "full new life" that animates all this landscape breathes also through him, and his fancy does fly to the place of peace, merely by speaking its name. The poet does not stand against the wind, as he did in section XV, and there is no more tension or distance here between consciousness and nature than between East and West, which sponsor equally the healing message.

In section LXXXIII, the poet has called on the spring to "delay no more" and to bring to him a form of release more obscure than any he receives in section LXXXVI. "What stays . . . thy sweetness from its proper place?" he asks, in the words that he will use in section CXVII to describe his longed-for and "proper place" in Hallam's embrace, and he looks to the spring-time for completion. This lyric, like LXXXVI, and, even more, like LXXXVIII, reaches out to a fullness just beyond its grasp, in particular to a fullness of utterance. But "peace" would be too tame and exclusive a word for the feeling that the poet seeks.

> O thou, new-year, delaying long,
> Delayest the sorrow in my blood,
> That longs to burst a frozen bud
> And flood a fresher throat with song.

If "delayest" is an imperative—and this seems the least awkward construction of the syntax—then the poet may be asking for help either in holding on to his sorrow, or in holding it back. If "delay-est" merely describes the action of the tardy spring-time, it still leaves unclear whether the poet calls for an abatement of sorrow or for its fuller throated expression or, perhaps, for the second to accomplish the first. This is not yet, at any rate, the flood of song that the poet looks forward to, nor is section LXXXVI a flood of song, but a call intensely whispered.

When the flood of spring song does come in section LXXXVIII, the song is not the poet's but the nightingale's, and it has not replaced sorrow, but absorbed it. The poet reaches outside himself and into the domain of Romantic nature poetry in his continuing quest for the good moment and the fullness of present knowing.

> Wild bird, whose warble, liquid sweet,
> Rings Eden thro' the budded quicks,
> O tell me where the senses mix,
> O tell me where the passions meet,
>
> Whence radiate: fierce extremes employ
> Thy spirits in the darkening leaf,
> And in the midmost heart of grief
> Thy passion clasps a secret joy:
>
> And I—my harp would prelude woe—
> I cannot all command the strings;
> The glory of the sum of things
> Will flash along the chords and go.

This lyric combines the direct address of *In Memoriam*'s earliest sections with a frank appeal for information. As in section XVI the poet inquires about the diverse emotions that may be tenants of a single breast, but here the mixture includes joy—the image of the clasp returns with this crucial difference—and represents an achievement rather than a problem. The poet himself, however, stands at some distance from this achievement. The joy seized in birdsong remains secret, and the poet must reach out to its origins, to the place where the contraries of emotional and physical experience mingle in a glorious sum.

He reaches appropriately in the direction of the nightingale. It was the bulbul, Persian cousin of the nightingale in Tennyson's 1830 poem, "Recollections of the Arabian Nights," that mingled in its song all of the world, including life and death. And it is Keats, of course, whose nightingale is heard behind both of these Tennysonian birds, singing from a world that does not know the separations of time. The world of *In Memoriam* seems to have fallen from that wholeness, but the tones of Eden still carry to it in the song of the nightingale. Emerging from darkness, that song testifies to the power of the imagination, and one place that the passions meet is in the bird's song itself, just as the senses mix in its liquid sweetness. The song signifies the existence of a realm in which worldly differences are reconciled, a realm that contains both the origin and the end of song.

Tracking the wild bird's song to its "midmost heart," the poet seeks out the place where the passions meet, but also the place that they come from. "Whence radiate": the phrase stands out because of its placement after what seemed a complete thought. A parallel construction appears in the Prologue, where the poet also asks for knowledge and for the reconciliation of difference:

> Let knowledge grow from more to more,
>   But more of reverence in us dwell;
>   That mind and soul, according well,
> May make one music as before,
>
> But vaster.

The stanza and the thought seem complete in the same moment, only to be succeeded by the last two words, which enlarge the meaning suddenly and strikingly. In these two words the poet begs that the fall from the age of faith into the age of science be rendered fortunate. He suggests a justification and a goal for all of history.

The poet of section LXXXVIII speaks from within history and addresses a singing bird rather than a distant God. He will not wait through history for an end to difference, but demands his knowledge of wholeness now, for the mingling promised by the bird's song is not a mingling of senses and passions only, but of past, present, and future. The poem insistently juxtaposes images of earliness and lateness, of budded quicks and darkening leaf. In the figures of the poet, the plant world can be blooming and fading at once, and in the song of the bird Eden carries into the present. Christopher Ricks notes the Miltonic sources of the phrases "fierce extremes" and "the sum of things,"[2] phrases that carry Milton into the present, too. And the diction and the stance of the first line recall the moment in "L'Allegro" when Milton thought to hear Shakespeare "Warble his native wood-notes wild." The poet of *In Memoriam* hears in the song of the nightingale the earlier, more elemental voice that Milton heard in Shakespeare and so hearkens back to an earlier moment of hearkening back. Searching the song of the nightingale for evidences of an Edenic, ahistorical realm that has somehow survived into history, the poet of section LXXXVIII repeats the efforts of earlier poets and so closes the difference between present and past.

Yet the third stanza emphasizes that such an achievement is hardly complete, and that a distance still separates the poet from the wild bird. Turning explicitly to his own powers of song, the poet laments still a failure of poetic control, a failure that works two ways. With an emphasis on "will," the last two lines continue the theme of *In Memoriam*'s earliest sections and complain that the poet cannot keep the glory of the sum of things out of his poem. Yet the lines also register a complaint that the mingled tones of glory cannot be held, but flash into being and then vanish.

In his analysis of birdsong, the poet separates out times as well as places and passions, and names separately the Eden that birdsong mingles with the natural processes of the present. Two faculties, two imaginative impulses coexist. One attempts to write history and the other to deny it, to reassemble in song what analysis has put in pieces and thus to match the condensed glory of the song of the nightingale. The poet's song in section LXXXVIII does indeed mingle joy and grief, but it expresses as well the puzzlement of the last stanza. Talking about "the glory of the sum of things," the poet evokes something else, his own nervous and expectant wonder.

The poet's fullest vision of the sum of things and the most celebrated account of the experience of transcendence in all of Tennyson's poetry comes in section XCV. Sitting in the garden on a late, still summer evening and reading the letters of his dead friend, the poet discovers a sudden glory (lines 33-44):

> So word by word, and line by line,
>   The dead man touch'd me from the past,
>   And all at once it seem'd at last
> The living soul was flash'd on mine,
>
> And mine in this was wound, and whirl'd
>   About empyreal heights of thought,
>   And came on that which is, and caught
> The deep pulsations of the world,
>
> Aeonian music measuring out
>   The steps of Time—the shocks of Chance—
>   The blows of Death. At length my trance
> Was cancell'd, stricken thro' with doubt.

As in section LXXXVIII the apprehension of the sum of things flashes into being and then goes. Section XCV differs sharply, nonetheless, from *In Memoriam*'s other moments of hope and power, because its experience of communion is more intense and more sweeping, but also because it grounds that experience more convincingly in the context of ordinary life. The trance comes unexpectedly, to be sure, but it does not come of nothing. Hallam's letters are its immediate and suggestive cause. Furthermore, although the trance is not sustained as the poet might wish, neither is it without effect. The poem closes (lines 62-64) in triumph:

> And East and West, without a breath,
> Mixt their dim lights, like life and death,
> To broaden into boundless day.

East and West, early and late, mingle in one image of glory. The image also prepares, however, for the advance of time, and section XCV lends its authority to both of the historical visions adumbrated in earlier sections of *In Memoriam*. It seems both to deny the passage of time and to glorify it as a progress into boundless day. The trance of section XCV is in the same paradoxical relation to time as the mystical experiences of Tennyson's youth that were its model, and we may look to these experiences to place section XCV more clearly in context.

"A kind of waking trance I have frequently had, quite up from boyhood, when I have been all alone." Hallam Tennyson gives his father's own record of the experience:

> This has generally come upon me thro' repeating my own name two or three times to myself silently, till all at once, as it were out of the intensity of the consciousness of individuality, the individuality itself seemed to dissolve and fade away into boundless being, and this not a confused state; but the clearest of the clearest, the surest of the surest, the weirdest of the weirdest, utterly beyond words, where death was an almost laughable impossibility, the loss of personality (if so it were) seeming no extinction but the only true life.[3]

The closest approximation to this experience in Tennyson's poetry occurs in "The Ancient Sage" (lines 229-34):

> for more than once when I
> Sat all alone, revolving in myself
> The word that is the symbol of myself,

The mortal limit of the self was loosed,
And past into the Nameless, as a cloud
Melts into heaven.

Other poems from throughout Tennyson's career, such as "The Mystic," "Armageddon," and "Timbuctoo," all written by 1830, and "De Profundis" of 1880, describe experiences that bear at least a family resemblance. The intense experience of selfhood carries the poet beyond selfhood, just as language carries him beyond language. Time seems an illusion (see, for instance, the portentous account of "The Mystic," who "hath felt / The vanities of after and before"), but then time resumes, and the only illusion was the fleeting belief that it would not.

Section XCV transforms this structure by incorporating it into the history of the poet's long inner struggle and of our own long acqaintance with the poet. Like all Tennyson's trances, this one is an event strangely out of time, yet it is also a significant event in a continuing narrative. The contest of placement set in motion by one of these trances—the intense moment that both contains and is contained by a history of moments—is paradigmatic of part-whole relations throughout *In Memoriam*, and the relationship of the trance to its immediate surroundings is a version of the relationships between the single lyric and the whole of *In Memoriam*, between private and incommunicable intensity and the public language into which it rises or falls.

Yet the intense moment in section XCV is not so neatly isolated. It survives as a potent influence on succeeding moments and it originates, first, in a particular experience of landscape and, second, in the experience of another person. Language still triggers the trance, but the extreme self-absorption of the poet's recital of his own name has been replaced in *In Memoriam* by his reading of Hallam's letters. The incantatory power of oral repetition yields to the stranger speech of writing. Yet the experience, though it now involves another subject, has hardly become social. Like section XV, this is a Romantic nature lyric, complicated and transformed (as, indeed,

many Romantic nature lyrics were) by the presence of a third force.
It is a Tennysonian lyric, too, and an *In Memoriam* lyric, and the
opening landscape is characteristic (lines 1-16):

> By night we linger'd on the lawn,
>   For underfoot the herb was dry;
>   And genial warmth; and o'er the sky
> The silvery haze of summer drawn;
>
> And calm that let the tapers burn
>   Unwavering: not a cricket chirr'd:
>   The brook alone far-off was heard,
> And on the board the fluttering urn:
>
> And bats went round in fragrant skies,
>   And wheel'd or lit the filmy shapes
>   That haunt the dusk, with ermine capes
> And woolly breasts and beaded eyes;
>
> While now we sang old songs that peal'd
>   From knoll to knoll, where, couch'd at ease,
>   The white kine glimmer'd, and the trees
> Laid their dark arms about the field.

We need only think of the opening lines of "Tintern Abbey," or
even of section XV, to feel how utterly domesticated this landscape
is and to measure the distance the poet has come. Night has fallen
and with it a great quiet. Natural appearances are but faintly legible
in the darkness, and the sound of the "far-off" brook is at once a
small-scale version of the "inland murmur" of waters that Words-
worth heard, and a marked variation upon the other far-off pros-
pects of *In Memoriam*. Far-off in space and not in time, the brook
is not longed for, but comfortably present on the margins of an
inclusive scene. This calm landscape is waiting for something, but
not, apparently, for the peal of songs that dies into the night without
effect. The opening line suggests a series of such nights and such
scenes, a spacious sameness that may frustrate expectation. But the

fifth stanza changes direction and a particular series of events emerges out of the night (lines 17-33):

> But when those others, one by one,
>   Withdrew themselves from me and night,
>   And in the house light after light
> Went out, and I was all alone,
>
> A hunger seized my heart; I read
>   Of that glad year which once had been,
>   In those fall'n leaves which kept their green,
> The noble letters of the dead:
>
> And strangely on the silence broke
>   The silent-speaking words, and strange
>   Was love's dumb cry defying change
> To test his worth; and strangely spoke
>
> The faith, the vigour, bold to dwell
>   On doubts that drive the coward back,
>   And keen thro' wordy snares to track
> Suggestion to her inmost cell.
>
> So word by word . . .

"All alone" seems a necessary, but a qualified condition. The pairing of "me and night" makes a virtual subject of the surrounding natural scene, but the "leaves which kept their green" quickly supersede nature as the poet's companion. The passage stresses the power of writing to bring speech out of silence and to defy change and time. Hallam's own example suggests, too, the importance of a certain kind of reading, of the penetration that forces its way through wordy snares. No longer is transcendence achieved through some primal, talismanic use of language. This passage explicitly honors the power of the written word to incarnate spirit and to hold it in readiness for the truly adequate reader. Writing enters the trance structure, because time has entered in a new way. In the days when "Thought leapt out to wed with Thought / Ere Thought

could wed itself with speech" (XXIII), the miracle of contact be-
tween persons took place in a moment. The later miracle exceeds
the earlier because in joining persons it joins present and past. A
process that unfolds in time—"word by word, and line by line"—
suddenly breaks the ordinary flow of time—"all at once"—and re-
leases the poet into an experience of eternity.

But in accordance with the paradox of the trance structure, the
eternal moment passes. Time, chance, and death are measured out
for the poet, but his experience has another driving rhythm, besides
that provided by the "Aeonian music," and he passes from stanza
to stanza, through the trance and out. Once on the other side, the
poet complains that his own language cannot reproduce the expe-
rience that Hallam's writing led him to (lines 45-48):

> Vague words! but ah, how hard to frame
>   In matter-moulded forms of speech,
>   Or ev'n for intellect to reach
> Thro' memory that which I became.

"Frame" is appropriate here, for it is through framing and setting
that the poet attempts to convey the force of an experience that he
cannot describe head-on. The language of the trance itself is the
least exciting in the poem, dragged down by the knowledge of its
own inevitable failure to capture the uncapturable experience. This
is in contrast to the effortless adequacy of the evocative and descrip-
tive language that opens the poem and surrounds its central stanzas
of vision. Emerging from his trance the poet emerges into an ap-
parently unchanged landscape (lines 49-52):

> Till now the doubtful dusk reveal'd
>   The knolls once more where, couch'd at ease,
>   The white kine glimmer'd, and the trees
> Laid their dark arms about the field.

With the perfect repetition of lines 14-16, the poet frames his
vision neatly, and the reader first assumes that no time has passed.
It remains dusk, and the trance has taken place in a moment en-

tirely out of time. But this "doubtful dusk" turns out to be the dawn, and the visionary moment has somehow elided the night. Either the poet's reading and then his trance have lasted for several hours or, in the subtler and stranger suggestion of the poem, they have reversed the flow of time and carry the poet backward into the glory of an earlier day. Using the same lines to describe two different moments, the poet creates for the reader the same fold in time that Hallam's letters created for him, and the coming dawn seems not just to end the night, but to undo it. Although "dusk" can mean the darkness just before dawn, it more commonly refers to twilight, and the "doubtful dusk" of the stanza above returns us to an earlier scene and seems another reversal of natural process. The breeze that is about to transform the landscape will not blow across it, but is rather "suck'd" from out of the distance—something is taken back, and the ordinary flow of things is again reversed. The only sure way to distinguish the dawn from a miraculous reversal of the sunset would be the appearance of light from the East, but the source of light in this dawn is carefully diffused. The language of the close passes beyond quiet precision into large and exciting effects (lines 53-64):

> And suck'd from out the distant gloom
> A breeze began to tremble o'er
> The large leaves of the sycamore,
> And fluctuate all the still perfume,
>
> And gathering freshlier overhead,
> Rock'd the full-foliaged elms, and swung
> The heavy-folded rose, and flung
> The lilies to and fro, and said
>
> 'The dawn, the dawn,' and died away;
> And East and West, without a breath,
> Mixt their dim lights, like life and death,
> To broaden into boundless day.

This spectacular dawn clearly exceeds the merely natural, although Tennyson would doubtless have been anxious to point out that East and West really do seem to mix their lights on those short, northern summer nights in which the darkness is never quite complete. Even then, however, the breeze does not speak distinctly to announce the dawn, nor does the dawn mingle life and death except under the pressure of the excited imagination. The stillness and sameness of the rural tableau yield to the onrush of the transforming breeze and that sameness is now revealed as miraculous. Sunrise and sunset are identified as if, in the words of "The Ancient Sage," "as if the late and early were but one."[4] Nearer at hand is the mingling of East and West, early and late, in the address of section CXXI to the morning and evening star:

> Sweet Hesper-Phosphor, double name
> For what is one, the first, the last,
> Thou, like my present and my past,
> Thy place is changed; thou art the same.

The cyclic repetitions of nature are made for an enthusiastic moment to correspond with an essential constancy in human experience, and present and past are one.

The persuasive enthusiasm of section XCV, however, is not merely, or even primarily, the result of the paradoxical affirmations of its last few lines, and it is not just the brilliant dawn, but the strange, rocking heaviness of the natural scene that impresses upon us the fullness of this moment. The poet's apprehension of simultaneity yields a version of Keatsian ripeness, though it is the displaced spring-time ripeness of stanza V of the "Ode to a Nightingale" rather than the fruitfulness of "To Autumn." The sycamore leaves are large, the elm is "full-foliaged," the rose is "heavy-folded," the breeze is "gathering." It gathers in order to blow fresher and harder, and the heaviness of the landscape finally measures only the strength of this breeze, whose extraordinary progress is registered in the close sequence of predicates: tremble, fluctuate, rocked, swung, flung, said, died. But death is not the end, and the breeze expends itself in announcing the boundless day. Fulfillment is thus succeeded by expectation, but the second neither contradicts nor cancels the first, and the lyric ends in excited satisfaction. The poet has emerged from one vision only to have another, and the intense moment of the trance has its effect in the moments that follow.

There is a tension, nevertheless, in this lyric, as elsewhere in *In Memoriam*, between the claims of the intense moment and the normalizing sequence of moments around it. Advancing from night into boundless day, the poet still must live in time, which means leaving himself open to all the chance and mischance of the future and leaving behind the absolute assurance of the moment of communion. He must leave behind "the living soul," too, and the ambiguity of this phrase introduces a second tension, parallel to that between the two visions of time. Early editions of the poem described a mystical encounter that was clearly with Hallam:

> And all at once it seem'd at last,
> His living soul was flash'd on mine,
>
> And mine in his was wound,

but in 1872 Tennyson changed the first "His" to "The" and the second to "this." Critics have generally approved the changes as lending an appropriate vagueness to the mystical experience,[5] but it is doubtful whether the first readings were not more truthful to the fierce and specific longing for reunion with Hallam that animates so much of *In Memoriam*. The "at last" of line 35 supports such a view, for previous sections have craved contact not with any great soul, but with a lost human friend. The elder Tennyson feared "giving a wrong impression" and explained that "The greater Soul may include the less."[6] The altered readings thus contribute to the development of an important theme in the poem, but this ought not to obscure the fact that the exact place of the lesser, individual soul remains an open and a crucial question. When the poet later mingles Hallam with all of nature, Hallam's is the greater soul, and nature diffuses but does not dissolve or overshadow his personality.

      I agree with most modern critics of *In Memoriam* that section XCV is the most ambitious and the greatest lyric in the poem, but admiration does not require religious conversion, and there is no need to take the poet's mystical experience as clinching evidence for the rightness of his affirmations in this and succeeding lyrics. The nature of its claim upon us and, indeed, of its effect upon the poet, is quite different from this. The poet himself does not argue from his trance or claim it as evidence of anything. He does make an apparent allusion to it in section CXXII, but he is far more cautious than I have been about claiming it as the cause of any later effect. And the language of the trance itself is more cautious and ambiguous than the headlong rush of events in section XCV at first permits us to notice. It can only be the tone of surrounding passages that makes us sure, for instance, that it is a good thing to catch "The deep pulsations of the world, / Aeonian music measuring out / The steps of Time—the shocks of Chance— / The blows of Death." Think how differently we read the emotional significance of the similar passage in section XXXV in which the poet hears (lines 9-12)

> The moanings of the homeless sea,
>   The sound of streams that swift or slow
>   Draw down Aeonian hills, and sow
> The dust of continents to be.

The deep pulsations of the world have been intermittently audible throughout *In Memoriam*, and the poet has ascended before to the empyreal heights, as in section LXXVI. Section XCV discovers no new philosophy or cosmology, nothing new about the way the universe is ordered, but only a new and deeply comforting experience of this order.

Nor is this experience as unavailably mystical as it might at first appear. We roll through line 35—"And all at once it seemed at last"—without pausing over the "seemed" that separates the achievement of "all at once" from the history of longing in "at last," and that furthermore separates the "dead man" of line 34 from the "living soul" of line 36. Such caution and precision draw the trance back toward its origins in the simple miracle and the *seeming* presences of reading. The "fall'n leaves which kept their green" (line 23) were already evidences of a power beyond nature, and the "silent-speaking words" (line 26) a sufficiently paradoxical and impossible achievement.

"A hunger seized my heart"; with these words the poet allies himself with another Tennysonian discoverer, Ulysses, whose "hungry heart" wanted more and more of knowledge and experience. For each of these characters the hunger of the heart is another near paradox, a voracious receptivity that is active and passive at once. The poet of *In Memoriam* has been passive before his moods all along, but he discovers in section XCV a wiser passivity and consents at last to read his visions rather than to write them. He has read himself before, and, reading "love's dumb cry defying change," he might be reading himself again, the noble letter of one of his own dead selves, the author of the earlier sections of *In Memoriam*. But in section XCV, for the first time, the poet-reader is not lamenting an irrecoverable past or invoking some dimly descried presence or trying to adjust himself honorably to the conflicting influences of the world and his grief. Instead, he reads himself and Hallam and the landscape without any feeling of loss or discrepancy, and his hunger is satisfied.

The mysterious and believable action of section XCV takes place within the poet, who suddenly discovers what he might have known already about the nature of his friend's survival. Although it celebrates the power of an immediate experience, section XCV ultimately embraces the mediations of language and natural appearances and satisfies itself with the renovation of spirit that language and landscape can both trigger and represent. Telling us that neither language nor memory can recover "that which [he] became" in his trance, the poet installs an absence at the center of his lyric, but then surrounds it with images of sufficiency. The limitations of matter-molded forms of speech are accepted, and we know as much as we need to about the poet's trance experience. Indeed, we know as much as he does, by the time he comes to write his account, and section XCV is one of the few lyrics in *In Memoriam* that is narrated in the past tense.[7] Without pretending to write from the moment, the poet stands outside the experience that he so satisfactorily relates, and thus expands the moment in another way, bringing into relationship the time of experience and the time of writing. There is no casting about for memories, no nervous distrust of the ability of language to capture anything but the one missing element, the trance itself, whose absence stands as an acknowledgment of limitation, but not of defeat. Language is enough in Hallam's letters, and the world is enough in the closing image of the dawn.

Our assent to section XCV is not an assent to mysticism, but to the vividness with which this experience of satisfaction is rendered. The indissoluble connections of the moment to other moments and of the self to an enclosing order are radically and successfully confirmed. But section XCV is a unique event in *In Memoriam*, never singled out by Tennyson himself as a turning point or even as a division between one section and another. If all that I have claimed for the lyric is true, then it is reasonable to ask why the poem does not end with it. The tentative answer must be that Tennyson is willing to grant no moment that sort of authority, that every lyric, but especially one so grand in its claims, must be contained and criticized by what succeeds it, and that the poet must survive into the coming day to report on the quality of his experience there.

5

THE
CONDITIONS
OF BELIEF

Although the avowed object of the poet's belief in
the closing sections of *In Memoriam* is a future and physical reunion
with his friend, the condition of belief is something else, a sense of
present well-being that is partly sponsored, we may guess, by the
trance of XCV, but that is also, like that trance, mysterious, from
beyond the will, a sign of grace. The poet's hopes for the future,
like his "passion of the past," are important to the poem as present
events, and the focus is not on those future moments in which
expectation is fulfilled, but on the present moments in which it is
sufficient, or even unnecessary, because the moment itself is suffi-
cient. The poet's notorious twin faiths, in the progress of the species
and in the life to come, are more often the hypotheses than the sure
foundation of his lightened vision of earthly life, and his achieve-
ment in these closing sections is less to inhabit the "boundless day"
of section XCV than to hold it within the reach of hope and memory.
He thus remains the poet of partings and greetings, gatherings and
fadings, recollections and presentiments.

For many readers, this closing movement of *In Memoriam* is its
least satisfactory, seriously flawed by all the quotable affirmations
of the cosmic order that have securely placed the poem as "Victo-
rian," in the still faintly pejorative meaning of that term. There are
weak lyrics in this section, especially those in which the poet thinks
how gloriously Hallam would have deserved "the grand old name
of gentleman" (CXI), and there are moments of exaltation that we

THE CONDITIONS OF BELIEF

may not know how to share, moments in which the problem of belief is sharply focused. But there are fewer of these, I think, than many readers have supposed, and there is still, even as the poem rises to its celebratory conclusion, sufficient variety and complexity of feeling to constitute a criticism of life, as well as the rightness and beauty of phrasing that memorably portray one experience of living.

If *In Memoriam* is "too hopeful" for us, as it was for Tennyson, this is less because the happier moods of the close are unpersuasive or unbelievable than because the poem is arranged to give them an illusory privilege of place. We cannot help thinking, as we read the poem through, that these are not just the moods in which the poet happens now to find himself, but rather the spiritual resting-place at which, after long struggle, he has arrived. And because of the potent influence of this sense of long-awaited arrival, it is both difficult and important to see how qualified and hesitant the poet's triumph of faith actually is, and how dependent upon the triumphs of feeling that must be won again in each new moment.

Even after the powerful and comfortable experience of section XCV, the poet must practice again and again the turn away from unhappiness that is also a dangerous turn from the past and, thus, a form of betrayal. Different moments yield different versions of a faith that is always susceptible to correction or restatement in the moment that follows. And even as the last lyrics of the poem make certain the healing of the poet's mood, they imperfectly suppress his continuing uncertainties, both about the course of the human future and about the precise terms of his own undoubted joy.

The poet does not record for us the moments that immediately succeed section XCV—there is no morning-after report, and sections XCVI and XCVII step away from the emotional particulars of the poet's experience to offer, "running comment[s] on life," in Tennyson's own phrase for XCVII.[1] Section XCVI defends "honest

THE CONDITIONS OF BELIEF

doubt" as the path to a strengthened faith and instances Hallam as a follower of this path, obliquely comparing him to Moses and the Israelites, who heard God's voice speaking from the clouds over Mt. Sinai. In its assurance that "Power was with him in the night" and in the handsome impersonality of the closing simile, section XCVI begins to consolidate its faith in the vision of XCV,[2] but the mood of excitement has nevertheless passed. In section XCVII, the poet returns to a slightly altered version of the metaphor of section LX, and casts himself as the humble and adoring wife of a husband who moves in a mysterious and enlarged sphere. But the vaguely grand claim for this husband that "he knows a thousand things" signals the final weakness of a lyric that cannot tell us what any of these things is. Both of these sections were late additions to the manuscript, probably written between 1848 and 1850 and originally presented in reverse order. Their chief effect, whether intended or not, is to absorb the force of XCV and to offer us a poet and a poem that are changed only subtly by XCV if they are changed at all.

Sections XCVI and XCVII do, however, share with XCV the positioning of Hallam as a spiritual guide. Although his influence is differently received from one of these lyrics to another, he is the poet's example and prompter in each, as he is also in section XCVIII, the concluding lyric of the seventh of the nine sections into which Tennyson told James Knowles that *In Memoriam* was divided. Section XCVIII was probably written in 1836 and addressed to Charles Tennyson, who was married in that year and who took a wedding trip to Vienna, the city where Hallam had died. In it the poet expresses his own unwillingness to visit Vienna or to believe that it is anything but the city of separation and death.

> I have not seen, I will not see
> Vienna; rather dream that there,
>
> A treble darkness, Evil haunts
>   The birth, the bridal; friend from friend
>   Is oftener parted, fathers bend
> Above more graves, a thousand wants

> Gnarr at the heels of men, and prey
> By each cold hearth, and sadness flings
> Her shadow on the blaze of kings.

Although written six or seven years before section XCV, this lyric comes after it in the finished order of the poem and these lines are thus made into the assertion of a continuing will to mourn. The poet's world, reseen and remade in the dawn of XCV, must apparently be remade again and Hallam's own words are once again the agents of change:

> And yet myself have heard him say,
>
> That not in any mother town
> With statelier progress to and fro
> The double tides of chariots flow
> By park and suburb under brown
>
> Of lustier leaves; nor more content,
> He told me, lives in any crowd,
> When all is gay with lamps, and loud
> With sport and song, in booth and tent,
>
> Imperial halls, or open plain;
> And wheels the circled dance, and breaks
> The rocket molten into flakes
> Of crimson or in emerald rain.

It is a strange passage, in which the poet does not seem to be remembering what he has heard, but seeing with his mind's eye a transformed Vienna, the scene of continuing life. His vision spreads out across the city to observe an ordered contentment that gathers force and breaks free in the last few lines. The poet is suddenly there, the dance unfolds before him, the fireworks explode, and then the energy diffuses into dreaminess as the sparks begin to fall. The kinship of this vision to dream or trance is further strengthened by the fact that Tennyson cannot have heard Hallam "say" anything about Vienna, for it was on his first visit there that Hallam died.

Furthermore, in the letter to Alfred and Emily Tennyson on which these stanzas appear to be based, Hallam does not at all celebrate the city as a place of contentment or describe the city in anything like the slightly wonder-struck detail of the poem.[3] The poet's puzzled and inconclusive turn from images of death to images of life—one of many such turns in the poem—is a scene in his own internal drama, clearly staged by Tennyson and placed here to demonstrate both the continuance and the continuing necessity of such movements of the spirit.

When the promised dawn finally does arrive, in section XCIX, it is the "dim dawn" of the anniversary of Hallam's death, a day that brings "memories of bridal, or of birth" to many, but memories of death to many others. Resolving to "count as kindred souls" all those other mourners, the poet announces that he is not yet ready to leave off his own mourning, but the terms and tone of this announcement signal an important shift from the mood of section LXXII, the last observance of Hallam's death day. The poet does not now struggle to express the uniqueness and particularity of his grief, but rather welcomes his absorption into the community of mourners. And in the balanced acknowledgment that this day is only arbitrarily a day of grief, he withdraws an earlier insistence on the grim sameness of things. This day is many different anniversaries for different people, and the mere profusion and variety of possible memories begin to liberate the day from its bondage to the poet's particular past.

In sections XCIX through CVII, the poet observes Hallam's death day, Christmas, the new year, and Hallam's birthday in near succession, and the paradoxical effect of this confused concentration of anniversaries is to constitute still another kind of break from the past and from the determining hold of previous lyrics. Although this sequence of lyrics crosses over a structurally important division at section CIV—in either the three-part or the nine-part version of the poem's structure, this lyric begins the last part—it seems nevertheless to hang together, and the relations between these different kinds of anniversary distract our attention and the poet's from the relations between any one of them and the past. Observing all these symbolically charged days at once, the poem is suddenly overdetermined in its structure and the reader can hardly sort out the different designs of the whole that are suggested by each of them. A new pattern is thus created that takes the poet from death to birth and from fall to late winter, with several spring-time lyrics just ahead, and this pattern, though it hardly conflicts with the spirit of the larger structure of the poem, seems for the moment to replace it as the object of our immediate attention. By focusing upon the incremental difference of one moment from the next, rather than upon the tragic and absolute difference of death, the poet maintains and prizes the gradualism of his own changes of mood. In large ways and small, the poet keeps making and repeating his own characteristically subdued version of the elegiac turn, and this sequence of lyrics is itself a closely calibrated collection of such closely calibrated turns.

In the small-scale triumphs of these lyrics, it is not death that the poet must confront and redeem, but the threat of any change or movement at all, for each of these anniversaries is a moment of passing or transition, rather than a recognition of painful discontinuity. These are also the lyrics in which the poet bids farewell to his childhood home, and sections C-CIII describe the Tennysons' move from Somersby in 1837. But this break with the past is also softened, presented as a gentle loosening of spirit from place. The poet evokes the intermingling of spirit and place (C),

> I climb the hill: from end to end
> Of all the landscape underneath,
> I find no place that does not breathe
> Some gracious memory of my friend;

only to imagine their separation as something painless and gradual (CI):

> Unwatch'd, the garden bough shall sway,
> The tender blossom flutter down,

> Unloved, that beech will gather brown,
> This maple burn itself away;
>
> . . . .
>
> Till from the garden and the wild
> A fresh association blow,
> And year by year the landscape grow
> Familiar to the stranger's child;
>
> As year by year the labourer tills
> His wonted glebe, or lops the glades;
> And year by year our memory fades
> From all the circle of the hills.

The violence of burning and lopping is contained and softened here by fluttering, gathering, fading. The tentacular death-grip of the yew has become the soft and breakable embrace of a nostalgic consciousness and its objects. The poet must contend still with the old fear of section I that all change is deathly (C):

> And, leaving these, to pass away,
> I think once more he seems to die.

To leave the boyhood home, to move forward at all, is to reenact loss, to pass away. But the harshness of earlier sections of the poem is gone, and the poet's persistent anxiety is absorbed for the moment in the portrayal of a calm and beautiful regret.

In section CIII, the last of the lyrics about the move from Somersby, the poet records a vivid dream and constructs a myth that helps to reconcile him to change:

> On that last night before we went
> From out the doors where I was bred,
> I dream'd a vision of the dead,
> Which left my after-morn content.

He dreams of a home centered on the veiled form of Hallam, but also of a dove that calls him away from this home to a waiting boat and then downriver to the sea. There he finds a great ship and on it his friend, now a living giant three times his former size. The poet falls on his friend's neck, the wind makes "music out of sheet and shroud" (line 54), drawing strength even from death, and the lyric ends as the ship moves "towards a crimson cloud / That land-like slept along the deep."

The poet produces in this dream a redemptive, but still an entirely personal, vision of time and of glorious progress. The "forward-creeping tides" (line 37) that bear him to the sea are clearly an image of temporal flow, an echo of the "forward-flowing tide of time" from Tennyson's 1830 poem, "Recollections of the Arabian Nights." And the images of the giant Hallam and the closing music combine the vaster music called for in the Prologue (lines 25-29) with the "vaster passion" vaunted in section CXXX, creating a myth of personal progress that respects the specificity of the poet's experience, while still identifying his own history with that of the cosmos. The poet's dream presents still another version of the fortunate fall, a version that justifies and reassures the poet in his acceptance of change. If he will believe wholly in this new myth, he may now abandon the dead form to which he has paid homage and emerge into the flow of time, secure that he commits no act of disloyalty and that he loses nothing that will not be restored him in greater measure.

The dream-vision of CIII leaves the poet content for a morning, he says, but it is only a dream, and its effect is less certain even than that of the trance of XCV. It offers the private myth that the poet still requires, one that assures his future reward, but it can only present its assurances obliquely, as allegory, and much of this allegory is of questionable value to poet and reader alike. The rhetorical and evocative power of CIII is not in its allegorical personages, but in its hallucinatory landscape and in the hushed, accepting calm with which this landscape is presented. After the separations of sections C-CII, section CIII presents an image of the new world as an improved repetition of the old, a world of blending grandeur where the clouds and the land are mixed together and where "roll'd the floods in grander space" (line 26).

But these images *are* hallucinatory, and the dream-vision must still make contact with the daylight of the poet's experience. It describes the course of the future rather than that of the past and so its version of personal history is tentative, susceptible to falsification by events and to challenge from the much less mellow mood and weather of later lyrics, such as CVI and CVII. The dream does have power, but it is the power of present experience rather than of prophecy. Like the trance of XCV, this dream strongly affects the poet and opens up an expansive vision of all time, but also like XCV it cannot grant that vision authority. The vision of history taken from a moment must expose itself to the successive moments of history.

What the poet begins to find in the new moment of section CIV is that he cannot so easily abandon his long resistance to change. This is the third Christmas lyric of the poem and, according to either of Tennyson's accounts of its structure, the beginning of the last of its groups of lyrics. The poet is indeed in a new place and in a new mood, but it is a mood that betrays all his accumulated suspicion of newness. He greets the "new unhallow'd ground" (CIV) of "the stranger's land" (CV) with an eerie calm—and "strangely falls our Christmas eve." Change appears now in its new and beneficent aspect:

> No more shall wayward grief abuse
>   The genial hour with mask and mime;
>   For change of place, like growth of time,
>   Has broke the bond of dying use.

But the change of grief is a highly charged subject, and it leads next to the forced and alarming wrongness of the tone of section CVI, a lyric that celebrates the New Year with near-hysterical over-insistence:

Ring out, wild bells, to the wild sky,
The flying cloud, the frosty light:
The year is dying in the night;
Ring out, wild bells, and let him die.

The pronoun refers to the year, but it is hard not to hear in that last line quite another note of liberation, a wish to let Hallam truly die and to be freed from the bondage of grief and morbid attachment. This is the wish for healing change that the poet first encountered and resisted in section I. Even though it is concealed here as a second meaning, and even though it is therapeutically predictable and understandable, it is hardly a wish that the poet or the poem can sponsor unequivocally or for long.

The unnerving unsteadiness of the poet's tone in section CVI thus gives way to the chastened and finely particular observations of section CVII:

It is the day when he was born,
A bitter day that early sank
Behind a purple-frosty bank
Of vapour, leaving night forlorn,

The time admits not flowers or leaves
To deck the banquet. Fiercely flies
The blast of North and East, and ice
Makes daggers at the sharpen'd eaves,

And bristles all the brakes and thorns
To yon hard crescent, as she hangs
Above the wood which grides and clangs
Its leafless ribs and iron horns

Together, in the drifts that pass
To darken on the rolling brine
That breaks the coast. But fetch the wine,
Arrange the board and brim the glass;

> Bring in great logs and let them lie,
>   To make a solid core of heat;
>   Be cheerful-minded, talk and treat
> Of all things ev'n as he were by;
>
> We keep the day. With festal cheer,
>   With books and music, surely we
>   Will drink to him, whate'er he be,
> And sing the songs he loved to hear.

This is among the most satisfying of the poem's evocations of domesticity, and the elegiac turn, beautifully modulated, is a turning inward and indoors to the solid and immediate comforts that the poet can rely upon. The honest vagueness of "whate'er he be" combines with the vividly cold and brittle sharpness of the day to suggest a world of trouble and uncertainty, and the poet defends himself by pulling back to the closest of defensible borders, the solid core of the hearth. The cheerful-mindedness that he calmly resolves upon is not only a defense against the cold, but a correction of the emotional excesses of section CVI, just as his keeping of the day at all is a defense against forgetful joy. A day that sinks rather than rises is a day that stubbornly refuses to break free of its origins.

The upward movement from section XCIX to section CVII, a movement from death-day to birthday and from sorrow to quiet cheer, is also a carefully limited movement, a keeping to earth of what might have been a flight. Section CVII complements XCIX and closes off this sequence of lyrics by refusing the transformations of grief that were foretold in the dream of section CIII and in the reckless freedom of section CVI. Rather than let his friend die, the poet joins with others to say, "We will keep the day." Rather than pursue a transfigured image of his friend into new and uncharted regions, the poet will stay within doors to "talk and treat / Of all things ev'n as he were by." Here, as elsewhere in the poem, the alternative to moments of ecstatic but private vision is to return once more to the prospect of all humankind. This the poet has already done in the intimations of kinship with other mourners and in his retreat to the sure and social comforts of section CVII. And now section CVIII absorbs this experience and emits it as doctrine, a program for the future:

> I will not shut me from my kind,
> And, lest I stiffen into stone,
> I will not eat my heart alone,
> Nor feed with sighs a passing wind:
>
> What profit lies in barren faith,
> And vacant yearning, tho' with might
> To scale the heaven's highest height,
> Or dive below the wells of Death?
>
> What find I in the highest place,
> But mine own phantom chanting hymns?
> And on the depths of death there swims
> The reflex of a human face.
>
> I'll rather take what fruit may be
> Of sorrow under human skies:
> 'Tis held that sorrow makes us wise,
> Whatever wisdom sleeps with thee.

The poet does not renounce sorrow or self-indulgence, but rather the private, metaphysical exploration that has accompanied them. The barren faith and vacant yearning that he now rejects are apparently the impulses behind the lyric intensities of sorrow and joy that other sections have recorded. Faith and yearning both reach toward something absent, something outside the range of quotidian experience, but the poet now declares that such reaching has never truly carried him beyond himself, and he chooses a surer path, one that eschews the heights and the depths, and pursues instead the wisdom that an accepting and worldly sorrow can yield. Through the exercise of an interpretive, critical faculty that now enters the poem under the name of wisdom, the poet seeks to organize, rather than to enlarge or intensify his experience. After the extraordinary experiences of sections XCV and CIII, he indulges an impulse for balance and reflection, for hierarchy and system. In so doing, he takes literally his own resolution from section CVII to "talk and treat / Of all things ev'n as he were by." In the first shock of his grief, the poet sought a temporary refuge in the fancy that his friend was alive, and he does the same in sections CIX to CXIV, which are an extended celebration of what Hallam would have been. The stated goal of these unreal and conventional fancies is to describe a model of human behavior for the poet and for the world, but their real effect is to distract the poet and to weaken the poem.

"Wisdom" is the central term of praise in these lyrics, and it is a quality attributed both implicitly and explicitly to Hallam, whose passion and force are disciplined and directed toward the enforcement of order. He is praised for his active powers, but even more for his powers of resistance, and it is all the forms of excess and disorder that must be resisted. When we are told that his keenness of intellect was a power "To strive, to fashion, to fulfil" (CXIII) the echo of the celebrated last line of "Ulysses"—"To strive, to seek, to find, and not to yield"—calls attention primarily to the differences between Hallam and that heroic quester. Knowledge is unruly—"Who shall fix / Her pillars" (CXIV)—while Hallam is himself "A pillar steadfast in the storm" (CXIII). In the language of section CXIV, Wisdom is opposed to Knowledge in terms that again recall Ulysses and Telemachus, and it is Knowledge that conducts the quest for experience:

> But on her forehead sits a fire:
> She sets her forward countenance
> And leaps into the future chance,
> Submitting all things to desire.

Knowledge must defer, however, to the regulating, measuring influence of Wisdom, for this lyric belongs to Telemachus: "A higher hand must make her mild, / If all be not in vain." In wishing that the world be more like the wise Hallam, the poet significantly connects the appropriate virtues with a decorous gradualism and an implied philosophy of progress:

> I would the great world grew like thee,
>   Who grewest not alone in power
>   And knowledge, but by year and hour
> In reverence and in charity.

The celebration, in these lyrics, of kinship, of gradual change, and of the known virtues is simultaneously a renunciation of the intense moment and of the quest for unattainable knowledge, for the answers that lie behind the veil.

Yet, as always, the anomaly within the system, the unrepentant desire for unique experience, asserts itself. A closer look at section CVIII reveals that the dismissal of mystical forays into the highest and the lowest was hedged with qualification, and even a first look at sections CIX-CXIV has revealed that there is little imaginative force behind the poet's new steadiness. We may admire Hallam's virtues without at all admiring Tennyson's presentation of them in these lyrics, and we may turn to the testimony of other lyrics to strengthen our case against this turning away from the dead Hallam—"whate'er he be" in favor of an extended dalliance with the Hallam who might have been.

In an earlier draft of section CVIII, the poet abandoned far more regretfully the pursuit of the secrets of the grave. In this first version, the composure and balance of the last two lines—" 'Tis held that sorrow makes us wise, / Whatever wisdom sleeps with thee"—was tipped dangerously and the lyric ended in irresolution: " 'Tis held that sorrow makes us wise / Yet how much wisdom sleeps with thee." Tennyson later used this couplet as the opening of section CXIII, but the sense is changed completely in this new context, and the couplet is not a question but a declaration, leading on to a consideration of the wisdom that Hallam would have displayed in life. The sense of earnest gazing into the depths of death is lost,

133

and Tennyson has impoverished section CVIII without enriching CXIII.

But even in its revised form, section CVIII registers obliquely the power of all that it intends to renounce. There is an implicit reservation, if not an explicit one, in the last line even as revised, and there is the evidence in both versions that the poet records a common assumption—" 'Tis held"—rather than a private conviction. And the concern for profit, for gathering the fruit of sorrow, recalls the rejected rhetoric and comfort of section I, as other of these late lyrics also will. The poet cannot calculate his own emotional gain without risking the harsh judgment of his earlier self. Most important and characteristic, there is the strange and unassimilable third stanza with its assertion that "on the depths of death there swims / The reflex of a human face." What this must mean in its context is that all the quasi-spiritualism of earlier sections of the poem is flawed by the poet's epistemological limitations, by his inability to encounter anything but his own projections. But the human face nevertheless shines out from these lines like a promise, and the image fascinates and attracts us more than anything else in the lyric. The poet cannot stay out of these depths for long.

After all the lyrics of praise for the Hallam who might have been, the poet offers us in section CXV a springtime lyric that is another form of accommodation to gradual change, but that is also a return to the radiant present. Although it examines the world of immediate appearances and not the heights or the depths, section CXV is nevertheless a rapt and asocial fancy. Past and future, fading and burgeoning, are condensed in the intensity of the moment, and the poet concentrates all his energy on the evocation of *now*.

> Now fades the last long streak of snow,
> Now burgeons every maze of quick

About the flowering squares, and thick
By ashen roots the violets blow.

Now rings the woodland loud and long,
    The distance takes a lovelier hue,
    And drown'd in yonder living blue
The lark becomes a sightless song.

Now dance the lights on lawn and lea,
    The flocks are whiter down the vale,
    And milkier every milky sail
On winding stream or distant sea;

Where now the seamew pipes, or dives
    In yonder greening gleam, and fly
    The happy birds, that change their sky
To build and brood; that live their lives

From land to land; and in my breast
    Spring wakens too; and my regret
    Becomes an April violet,
And buds and blossoms like the rest.

The poet of section XVIII had looked forward at Hallam's grave-
side to the time when "from his ashes may be made / The violet of
his native land." In the first and last stanzas of this lyric, the trans-
formation is symbolically accomplished and even the poet's regret
is absorbed into the process of renewal. But the undeniable affir-
mation and animation of this welcoming of the springtime conjoin
oddly with a sense of trancelike compression and stillness. The
poet's regret in the last stanza is not merely healed by the landscape,
but converted into landscape, and there is no longer any separation
between what the poet sees and what he feels. Until the mention of
"my regret" in the last stanza, there has been no first-person sin-
gular at all in the poem, and the scene before the poet's eyes has
not been set over against his registering consciousness, but simply
presented as an immediate object of the senses.

The elements of the scene are themselves strangely intransitive, caught in a fullness of being that blurs the distinction between subject and object or between agent and activity. The lark drowns in its element and becomes its song. "Sightless" does not mean blind, as we would expect, but unseen—it is we who are without sight of the bird, and the adjective has distributed its influence over the perceiver and the perceived. The sky is living, the woodland itself is ringing, and the milky sails are described not in motion but in the process of becoming more intensely themselves. Even the migration and the procreation of the birds is rendered as a form of absorbed stillness. They do not go from one place to another, in the language of the lyric, but "change their sky"—as if the world revolves around them—and "live their lives / From land to land" within an enclosure of repetitions. Here, as elsewhere in *In Memoriam*, the verbal formula "*x* to *x*" turns an expanse into an encirclement.

The poet is not exploring the depths of death in section CXV, or rejecting wisdom in favor of knowledge, but he is indulging the habit of mind that is elsewhere responsible for such explorations and that seeks an encounter, now and face to face, with that which is. Section CXV leads on to CXVI, with its decisive turn from retrospection to anticipation—

> Yet less of sorrow lives in me
> For days of happy commune dead;
> Less yearning for the friendship fled,
> Than some strong bond which is to be.

—and to the celebrations of progress in CXVII and CXVIII, which I want next to examine. But there are different moods of satisfaction in the late lyrics of *In Memoriam*, and to the most intense and memorable of them the anticipation of progress would be an injury, as any anticipation at all would be a needless distraction. Section CXV is of this kind. It greets the coming spring, but does not itself look forward, and its deeper affinity is not with those other lyrics that seek their fulfillment in the future but with such celebrations of repetition and simultaneity as sections CXIX and CXXI and CXXIII.

First, however, the poet does work another vein of feeling and of speculation, and I do not mean to condescend to his faith in the future or to ignore his performances as laureate. They are dignified and moving performances, and it is a compellingly and variously expressed faith, to which the relevant challenge is offered not only by other lyrics and by our own skepticism, but also by the professing lyrics themselves. In section CXVII, for instance, the poet's hopeful account of the effects of time and change, is offered, as so often, in a subversively suggestive form:

O days and hours, your work is this
To hold me from my proper place,
A little while from his embrace,
For fuller gain of after bliss:

That out of distance might ensue
Desire of nearness doubly sweet;
And unto meeting when we meet,
Delight a hundredfold accrue,

For every grain of sand that runs,
And every span of shade that steals,
And every kiss of toothed wheels,
And all the courses of the suns.

The poet answers here his own question from section I, "But who shall so forecast the years / And find in loss a gain to match," and the answer is that it is no longer a hard question. The poet subscribes readily to the cheerful economy of gains and accruing delights, and his confidence in the future is an unexamined fact of life. But although the poem is clearly underwritten by this confidence, the facts of life that it actually does examine are quite different. The first two stanzas have the world so well figured out that they seem to be feeling nothing at all, neither desire nor imagined delight, and the poet is just settling back for the long wait before proper life begins. But the last stanza has a suddenly vivid sense of its subject, which is not, however, the infinitude and inevitability of delight, but the concretely and ubiquitously registered advance of time. In the fascinated figures of the first three lines, the poet blinks from one image of this advance to another, as time runs and steals and ticks forward, both in the large movements of nature and in the tiny moving parts of a watch. Then, as we move from every to every, to every to all, the last line opens outs into an immensity of space and time that could hardly be filled by any imaginable experience of delight. Certainly it is not delight that the lyric imagines most fully or whose image it leaves finally before us, and the poet has said no more of his own joyous future than that he expects it to come.

An easier way to fill the yawning gap of future time is with a narrative of universal progress, and, in section CXVIII, the poet turns outward to the history of the earth and of the species to discover a context for his own drama of grief and recovery and to begin construction of the large vision of human history that appears in the Epilogue. "Contemplate all this work of Time" is the command that opens up the grand view:

> . . . They say
> The solid earth whereon we tread
>
> In tracts of fluent heat began,
>   And grew to seeming-random forms,
>   The seeming prey of cyclic storms,
> Till at the last arose the man;
>
> Who throve and branch'd from clime to clime,
>   The herald of a higher race,
>   And of himself in higher place,
> If so he type this work of time
>
> Within himself, from more to more;
>   Or, crown'd with attributes of woe

Like glories, move his course, and show
That life is not as idle ore,

But iron dug from central gloom,
    And heated hot with burning fears,
    And dipt in baths of hissing tears,
And batter'd with the shocks of doom

To shape and use. Arise and fly
    The reeling Faun, the sensual feast;
    Move upward, working out the beast,
And let the ape and tiger die.

This is the self-conscious laureate at his best, forging a scientifi-
cally precise and poetically powerful account of the earth's creation,
and then relating that account, through argument and metaphor, to
the particular and human story his poem has recorded. He has
suffered, in Hallam's death, the shocks of doom (cf. XVI, line 11,
and LXXXV, line 55), and he describes his own spiritual recovery in
a geographical vocabulary that does justice to both realms. There
remains, however, a subversive strain within this happy reconcilia-
tion of spirit and science, of individual experience and its racial
model. The introductory formula, "They say," receives no special
emphasis, but is a reminder nonetheless that this wisdom is re-
ceived from without rather than proved from within. The image of
man as precursor to some higher version of himself appears without
comment, but must be set against Tennyson's remark to John Ster-
ling, as reported by John Tyndall: "I should consider that a liberty
had been taken with me if I were made simply a means of ushering
in something higher than myself."[4] One trusts the tale and not the
teller, but even the tale registers subtle reservation. Man will pre-
pare the way for higher beings only if he repeats this progressive
pattern in his own life, and such a repetition relies on an exploita-
tion of grief that the poet has severely criticized in earlier sections.
To be "crown'd with attributes of woe / Like glories" goes beyond

the resolve to earn wisdom from sorrow and makes a show of mourning.

I may be wrong in this reading, of course, and the poet may intend no more than the glorification of man's power to draw good from evil. The theory of progress can justify its own ascendancy here by claiming that the poet has progressed to the point of embracing it. The truly forceful argument against such a secure notion of progress appears in the lyrics that conclude *In Memoriam*, lyrics that reveal a decided return to an earlier valuation of the private and the mystical, and that put aside sweeping historical vision in favor of the continued and, necessarily, the perpetual effort to redeem the present and find it sufficient.

One way that later lyrics implicitly challenge the poet's representative and generalizing faith in the future is by their reminder that a common faith is not more secure than the act of assent that the individual offers it. The poet of *In Memoriam* never believes quite as resoundingly and persuasively in what "they say" as in what he idiosyncratically feels. He instructed the reader in an earlier stanza of section CXVIII to "trust that those we call the dead / Are breathers of an ampler day / For ever nobler ends," and the vagueness of the object of this trust is matched by the weakness of "trust" itself, a word that is always ready in *In Memoriam* to be diminished—the poet "can but trust" in LIV and "faintly trust[s]" in LV— in the presence of strong feeling. What the poet names as trust must either be supported or swept away by inward conviction. In section CXX, he offers resistance to the world of public and objective report, with which he was temporarily allied in CXVIII, and announces his intention to abandon what "they say" whenever it swerves from what he feels.

> I trust I have not wasted breath:
> I think we are not wholly brain,
> Magnetic mockeries; not in vain,
> Like Paul with beasts, I fought with Death;

Not only cunning casts in clay:
Let Science prove we are, and then
What matters Science unto men,
At least to me? I would not stay.

Let him, the wiser man who springs
Hereafter, up from childhood shape
His action like the greater ape,
But I was *born* to other things.

The poet stands alone, deepening his nervous trust into conviction. To have wasted breath would mean to have wasted life, to have found no use, after all, in the "blood and breath" of section XLV. It would also mean to have wasted the effort invested in the creation of *In Memoriam*. But the poet simply, and not at all shrilly, insists that he has not wasted his breath, and that closing note of defiance anticipates the famous assertion of the heart, "I have felt," from section CXXIV. It is significant, too, that his assurance derives not from any putatively observed fact about the future of the species, but from the welling up in the present of his own deep certainty. Indeed, the poet looks ironically on the wiser man of the future and thus questions the brand of evolution described in CXVIII. Although Tennyson's note to this lyric for the Eversley edition makes clear that its target is materialism, rather than evolution, the poet is nevertheless so skeptical of the progress of the species that he imagines a resemblance and a chain of connection between the apes of the past and the supermen of the future, a chain from which he, in the present, must break free. That emphatic, *"born,"* furthermore, counters a progressivist emphasis on the gradual making of the species and confirms the determining power of origins over ends, of the birthright that the poet senses and claims for himself over the "far-off" events of the human future that may be divine or not, but whose divinity the poet cannot *know* as he knows himself.

In section CXX, the poet emphatically rejects the historical argument that looks to the future for the justification of the present. But this is not a denial of history or of motion. To be "born to" something is to feel within an urging toward the future, the intimations of a career and a destiny in time. Reviewing the course of his own journey through the poem, the poet cannot help knowing and believing in at least one form of progress, which is the gradual healing of his own mood. But he must have complicated reservations about this progress, too, and from the first lyric of *In Memoriam*, the poet has identified the kinds of change that he might undergo in his career as a mourner with the terrible change that he has undergone in becoming a mourner. Section CXX answers the historical optimism of section CXVIII by disclaiming interest in the future of the species. Section CXIX, meanwhile, has attempted in another way to vindicate the present, by taking up the charged question of the poet's relationship with the personal past. Repeating the words, as well as the setting, of an earlier lyric, the poet shows how differently the same situation may be experienced and calls attention to the complexities that make it impossible to say any one true thing about this relationship. The debate between constancy and change is renewed in this lyric, but the poet has more choices now than to grieve forever or to be "crown'd with attributes of woe / Like glories," as he was in CXVIII. This is one in a series of late lyrics in which the poet returns to the mood of section CXV, seeking to recover the sense that the present is full and sufficient.

> Doors, where my heart was used to beat
> So quickly, not as one that weeps
> I come once more; the city sleeps;
> I smell the meadow in the street;
>
> I hear a chirp of birds; I see
> Betwixt the black fronts long-withdrawn
> A light-blue lane of early dawn,
> And think of early days and thee,

> And bless thee, for thy lips are bland,
>   And bright the friendship of thine eye;
>   And in my thoughts with scarce a sigh
> I take the pressure of thine hand.

This lyric clearly repeats and revises section VII:

> Dark house, by which once more I stand
>   Here in the long unlovely street,
>   Doors, where my heart was used to beat
> So quickly, waiting for a hand . . .

Absorbing, reordering, and revising the phrases of the past, the poet now answers the negations of section VII and triumphs over the discontinuities that earlier caused such pain. This is a triumph, too, of the creating imagination over all the forms of absence imposed by the world. In the words of James Kincaid, section CXIX "celebrate[s] the power of the newly found self—'I come,' 'I smell,' 'I hear,' 'I see,' 'I take.' "[5] The poet's vision mends the break between man and nature by mingling the sights and sounds and smells of the country with the dismal, urban scene of VII. More important, he mingles present and past in his thoughts of early days, and in the most striking contrast with section VII, he "takes the pressure" of the hand that he earlier said could be clasped no more. But the significance of these changes is not simply that the poet now feels better, though this is surely true, or that he now grasps the hand that he once waited for, for this is only half-true. He takes his friend's hand as he always has taken it—"In my thoughts"—and the saving difference is not just in the physical force of this memory, its "pressure," but in the fact that he can remember now with "scarce a sigh." It is not the vividness with which the past is recovered, but the pleasure, that marks the poet's new self.[6] Memory is healed, and the distance between the present and the past is negotiated not by magic or mysticism, but by the acceptance of memory's terms.

Given these terms, it is hardly clear whether this lyric stresses more emphatically the inevitability or the impossibility of repeating the past. The poet comes "once more" to Hallam's door in both section VII and section CXIX, and the second "once more" both repeats the first and leap-frogs over it to make a better, truer connection with some original event. Repeating the "once more" of section VII, section CXIX, joins the earlier moment in shared exile from the past that really matters. Leaping over it to take the pressure of Hallam's hand, even in thought, the poet closes the gap between himself and Hallam only at the expense of acknowledging a gap between the inconsolable mourner of VII and the satisfied rememberer he vowed never to become. In either event, the poet finds his comfort not in a new and arguable belief about the future, but in a new way of taking the objectively unchanged facts of the present.

In sections CXXI-CXXIII, the poet finds or seeks still other ways for imagination to charge the present with significance and to negate or make irrelevant the passage of time. These are among the finest of the late lyrics of *In Memoriam*, and thus among the most properly influential in setting its tone. And none of them expresses a faith, or even an interest, in the future. For them, as for section CXIX, the relevant afterlife is the afterlife of past events in the present, and ghosts are only some among the many marginal presences that appear to consciousness. The crucial gesture of faith is the one that the poet extends toward his own imaginative projections, of whom the ghost of Hallam is only one. The most memorable and imposing accomplishment of these lyrics is to make real, not the ghost of Hallam, but a comfortable and inclusive image of the present world, an image that the poet conjures up and then believes in.

Section CXXI concentrates on capturing in the present all the intimations of life just past or just beginning. For Gerard Manley Hopkins, the lyric was a touchstone, and he interrupts a discussion of Tennyson's limitations to quote from it and to admonish his correspondent: "Surely your maturest judgment will never be fooled out of saying that this is divine, terribly beautiful:"[7]

> Sad Hesper o'er the buried sun
> And ready, thou, to die with him,
> Thou watchest all things ever dim
> And dimmer, and a glory done:
>
> The team is loosen'd from the wain,
> The boat is drawn upon the shore;
> Thou listenest to the closing door,
> And life is darken'd in the brain.
>
> Bright Phosphor, fresher for the night,
> By thee the world's great work is heard
> Beginning, and the wakeful bird;
> Behind thee comes the greater light:
>
> The market boat is on the stream,
> And voices hail it from the brink;
> Thou hear'st the village hammer clink,
> And see'st the moving of the team.
>
> Sweet Hesper-Phosphor, double name
> For what is one, the first, the last,
> Thou, like my present and my past,
> Thy place is changed; thou art the same.

For the poet, as for the migrating birds of section CXV, history is a change of sky, a revolution of the heavens around a still, central point. The past is not identified with the future, as the doctrine of some past lyrics would suggest, but with the present, and what the poet knows and affirms is that all moments are of the same transitory and marginal character. Continuing human life is not evoked here as a consecutive progress from beginnings to endings, but rather as the fading and brightening of a consciousness that is at once cosmic and domestic. The poet who watches the evening star

145

imagines that the star is watching back, conferring on all the sights and sounds that he records the significance of heavenly regard. But this significance is finally and confessedly personal, and it is the identity of "*my* present" and "*my* past" that the turning of the earth confirms. Like the "dying ears" and "dying eyes" of "Tears, Idle Tears," the consciousness of section CXXI is generalized, but distinctly human, and "the world's great work" is glimpsed or overheard by a central awareness that is attributed to the star, but that seems, in lines 7-8 and 10-11, to be indoors and in bed.

Glimpsing and overhearing, slipping into and out of sleep, this awareness is thus both central and marginal at once, participating in nothing, but relating all things to itself, bridging the gap between the dusk and the dawn without confronting the night or occupying the day. Like "Tears, Idle Tears," and like much of the rest of *In Memoriam*, section CXXI takes place on the thresholds of dawn and dusk. The sun is always just the other side of the horizon, the lyric is melancholy as well as peaceful, and the poet affirms the constancy and the continuity, but not the fullness, of human life.

But the fullness of life is nevertheless something that can be imagined and invoked and that is by no means the property of the legendary past or the legendary future. For section CXXII, the present and the past are not the same, but they might be at any moment, and, in an apparent reference to the experience of section XCV, the poet asks for the repetition of an earlier, entranced moment. It is not sufficient to analyze and to reflect upon such experiences, for they are doubtful in memory. The poet wants the experience now, because that is the way to be sure he has had it at all:

> Oh, wast thou with me, dearest, then,
>> While I rose up against my doom,
>> And yearn'd to burst the folded gloom,
> To bare the eternal Heavens again,
>
> To feel once more, in placid awe,
>> The strong imagination roll

A sphere of stars about my soul,
In all her motion one with law;

If thou wert with me, and the grave
Divide us not, be with me now,
And enter in at breast and brow,
Till all my blood, a fuller wave,

Be quicken'd with a livelier breath,
And like an inconsiderate boy,
As in the former flash of joy,
I slip the thoughts of life and death;

And all the breeze of Fancy blows,
And every dew-drop paints a bow,
The wizard lightnings deeply glow,
And every thought breaks out a rose.

Like CXIX, this lyric juxtaposes the present with at least two different moments of the past and attempts to recapture an earlier experience of recapturing. Trying to figure out just which earlier events are alluded to in the "then" of line 1 and the "once more" of line 5, A. C. Bradley is provoked to eight pages of puzzled and finally unsatisfied commentary. He ends up with a best guess that the "then" refers to an amalgam of sections XCV and LXXXVI and that the earlier experience these lyrics revived for the poet was the generalized experience of youthful reassurance and joy that he owed to the living Hallam. But he concedes the uncertainty and the difficulties of this explanation, particularly the difficulty in taking "former flash of joy" to refer to a time of life rather than to a single intense experience. And, as Bradley also notices, the phrase "placid awe" does not seem appropriate to the excitement of XCV. Indeed, "placid awe" seems far closer to the mood of lyrics immediately surrounding CXXII, and, although I cannot tie up all of Bradley's loose ends without unraveling new ones, I would call attention to the similarities between the forms of imaginative exertion that this lyric describes and the achievements of sections CIII, CXV, CXIX-CXXI, and CXXIII.[8]

The poet rises up against his doom repeatedly in *In Memoriam*, but the phrase seems particularly apt as an account of the instinctive resistance to materialism that wells up in CXX and that will render him not just unwilling, but unable, to abandon his dream in the last line of CXXIII—"I cannot think the thing farewell." For the strong imagination to roll the sphere of stars about the poet's soul both anticipates the rolling deep of section CXXIII and recalls the revolving heavens of CXXI. And it also recalls the image of section CIII, where "roll'd the floods in grander space." In all of these images, as in the wondrous springtime of section CXV, it is the poet's own strong imagination that envisions and casts the creation in vast, mingling motion. The whole world is made meaningful in an act of transforming apprehension.

But this act is also, in some of its forms, surrounded by doubt and made explicitly to depend upon the giant "If" of section CXXII, line 9—"If thou wert with me and the grave / Divide us not." As in section XCV, the poet celebrates an experience that he must strive for and can lose. The call to Hallam, "Be with me now, / And enter in at breast and brow" recalls the uncertain "Be near me" of section L and the trance-invoking "Descend, and touch, and enter" of section XCIII, but the spirit of Hallam is not made by the language of this lyric to touch the poet as it did in sections XCV and CXIX.

And yet, even without this appearance of the living spirit, section CXXII invokes its imaginative transformation in language that is itself so vivid and excited that the job is almost done. The "flash of joy" and "the breeze of Fancy" recall from XCV both the trance itself, in which the "living soul was flash'd on mine," and the transforming breeze that followed it. But it is now the poet's own emotion that flashes upon him, and the spiritualist claims of earlier lyrics have given way entirely to the imaginative claims of Romantic landscape, claims whose basis in imagination is only made more explicit by the fact that they are expressed here in the form of desire rather than accomplishment. If the lyric seems nevertheless to record an experience of gratification, it is because desire becomes accomplishment through the power of Tennyson's language and through the unbroken intensity of the poet's attention to what he wants. And what he wants, judged by the distribution of this attention, is less the entry of Hallam than the consequent exaltation of his own spirit. The image of his blood rising up in "a fuller wave" seems to make a world of the strong self, just as the ambiguity of lines 5-7 allows the strong imagination not just to roll the sphere of stars, but to roll like a sphere of stars, a vast inner space. Finally, as "every thought breaks out a rose," the poet's exfoliating imagination both enters the world and appropriates it. The world is made thought, and thought is made real.

The most ambitious of the poet's appropriating acts of imagination, and the clearest response to the scientific speculations of section CXVIII, occurs in section CXXIII.

> There rolls the deep where grew the tree.
>   O earth, what changes hast thou seen!
>   There where the long street roars, hath been
> The stillness of the central sea.
>
> The hills are shadows, and they flow
>   From form to form, and nothing stands;
>   They melt like mist, the solid lands,
> Like clouds they shape themselves and go.
>
> But in my spirit will I dwell,
>   And dream my dream, and hold it true;
>   For tho' my lips may breathe adieu,
> I cannot think the thing farewell.

The long view of history results ultimately in a subordination of all to spirit, and this is not only the most ambitiously inclusive of the poet's visions of the world, but the most explicit about its own status as a created object. The poet does not stand inside history, but above and outside it, seeing it all, and the paradoxical effect of this embracing vision is to reveal all change as superficial and to equate the changes of geological time with the blending of all things accomplished by the poet's imagination. Forms change, but the poet can say to each of them, as he has to Hesper and Phosphor, "Thy place is changed; thou art the same." His vision mingles all that he sees or has seen or can imagine. The long noisy street of section VII recurs here, but loses its distinctness. The lands that are like clouds answer the "cloud / That landlike slept along the deep" in the dream of CIII. This, after all, is also a dream, and in the brazen assertion of the final stanza, the poet grants his dream the only epistemological authority there is.

It is just this calm assumption of authority that enables the poet to take on as his own the obliterating power of time and to present the transformation of the earth as the work of imaginative vision. The line in section CXXII, in which the imagination works "In all her motion one with law," describes this special form of power and the way in which the poet allies himself with the workings of the cosmos. But he is not passive in this alliance—authority is not passive—and it is the work of Tennyson's imagination that gives to the accounts of these grand workings their persuasive excitement and force. The poet of section LIV also dwelt in his dream, but had to ask a further question: "So runs my dream: but what am I?" The "I" of *In Memoriam* is now a strong source, and as its feelings have acquired the shape and finish of dreams, its dreams have acceded to the long-established authority of feeling.

Yet for all the seeming finality of the closing gesture of section CXXIII, *In Memoriam* has not spoken its last word. The privileged view of the self from the center of things must always be juxtaposed with another image that puts its privilege in question and that notices its insularity. The all-determining consciousness of section CXXIII stands outside the history of everything except itself, and its own changes remain mysterious. The self may assert its power over time and change, but an earlier record survives to expose that assertion as the evidence of change and, thus, as its potential victim. At the same time, the honesty of Tennyson's imagination keeps the poet from claiming too much or from pretending that he grounds this assumption of power in anything outside himself. To dwell in a dream knowingly and to hold it true arbitrarily could as easily be an enfeebled as an empowered gesture, and there is nothing except the poet's calm to keep us from taking the "but" of line 9 as a signal of retreat. The strange vagueness of the last line, which describes the power of resistance negatively, as an inability to surrender, leaves the poet in puzzled possession of a "thing" that is good to have, but that it would surely be reckless to name as love, or joy, or Hallam.

It would be more reckless still, then, to identify the vague "thing" of section CXXIII with a belief in the eventual perfection of humanity or in eternal life. And yet, if sections CXIX-CXXIII do not step forward in confident joy to advertise the benefits of history and society or the promise of heaven, neither do they refuse the consolations of an essentially secure vision of the cosmos. The last lyrics of *In Memoriam*, both those that we have just examined and the eight that follow them, are not divided between despair and good cheer or between grief and forgetfulness, but between different forms of reconciliation to the terms of life.

Just as it was possible in earlier lyrics for misery to express itself through the contemplation of sameness or of change, so it is possible now for the poet to take comfort in the prospect of the future and of the species or in the fullness and enclosure of a moment. It matters less whether the poet looks forward to the perfection of the species or to his own eternal life than that he looks forward at all. And it matters less, ultimately, whether he looks forward to the future or outward in the moment, than that he finds somewhere the better mood that both sponsors and is sponsored by belief. Such moods are both unarguable and vulnerable, and we judge them not by the soundness of the arguments that have produced them but by the power with which they are presented.

Although no later lyric has quite the power of CXXIII, all of them together compose an intriguingly shaded portrait of the final state of the poet's feeling and belief. Indeed, this belief is often so baldly and merely asserted, so much at odds with the particular observations of life that surround it, that the poet seems to be drawing attention to the fact that he has simply decided to believe and grounded his decision in nothing but feeling. And for all the prestige it has acquired in the course of the poem, feeling may still collapse into *mere* feeling at any turn, as it does in the course of this retrospective account in section CXXIV (lines 9-17):

> If e'er when faith had fall'n asleep,
>   I heard a voice 'believe no more'
>   And heard an ever-breaking shore
> That tumbled in the Godless deep;
>
> A warmth within the breast would melt
>   The freezing reason's colder part,
>   And like a man in wrath the heart
> Stood up and answer'd 'I have felt.'
>
> No, like a child in doubt and fear;

The heart does recover its strength in this lyric, but only because it is like a child that, "crying, knows his father near." Looking backward, the poet credits his spiritual progress not to his own strong feelings or to his decision to rely upon them, but to divine intervention: "And out of darkness came the hands / That reach thro' nature, moulding men." But Hallam's hands get mixed up here with God's, and the lyric never gets its divinity any more clearly in focus than it had in the first stanza, which cast about blindly for the object of its prayer:

> That which we dare invoke to bless;
>   Our dearest faith; our ghastliest doubt;
>   He, They, One, All; within, without;
> The power in darkness whom we guess.

After the strong and contained statements of sections CXIX-CXXIII, this lyric attempts to place feeling in context, by looking back over the whole movement of the poem to see the history that surrounds single moments and the divine agent that overlooks and guides the single self. But the attempt fails, because the poet cannot imagine God as a separate and distinct being or as anything more than a necessary hypothesis. God is defined here by the statements we make about him—He is "That which we dare invoke to bless"— and by the evidences of his activity in human lives: that the poet's life has taken a shape suggests the existence of a shaper; that the poet feels sometimes like a child suggests the existence of a father. The poet rejects the argument from design in this lyric—"I found Him not in world or sun, / Or eagle's wing or insect's eye"—only to substitute for it an argument from hazy inference. The final effect of this rather scattered argument is not to revoke the authority of feeling in favor of a higher Author, but merely to confirm that there are strong feelings and weak ones and that there is little force or clarity to the poet's present intuition of a power outside himself. Tennyson was bluffly forthright about the lack of nourishment provided by Matthew Arnold's humanistic theology in *Literature and Dogma*: "Matthew Arnold—'Something outside of us that makes for righteousness'—ugh!"[9] But in section CXXIV he does little better.

Other late lyrics proclaim a faith that is similarly enfeebled by vagueness or by peculiarities of emphasis. A vague faith may be strong, of course, and Tennyson's vagueness is a form of honesty, rather than of evasion. But what the poet's honesty keeps compelling us to discover in these last lyrics is that the poet's faith is simply and arbitrarily willed. He announces in section CXXVI that "Love is and was my King and Lord / And will be," and that he can hear "at times" a sentinel of this lord whispering, "In the deep night, that all is well." These are strong and comfortable words, but they are quickly and dangerously over-matched, in the next lyric, by the poet's honest consideration of the horrible prospect that the reassuring message is meant to face down (lines 9-20):

> But ill for him that wears a crown,
> And him, the lazar, in his rags:

> They tremble, the sustaining crags;
> The spires of ice are toppled down,
>
> And molten up, and roar in flood;
> The fortress crashes from on high,
> The brute earth lightens to the sky,
> And the great Aeon sinks in blood,
>
> And compass'd by the fires of Hell;
> While thou, dear spirit, happy star,
> O'erlookst the tumult from afar,
> And smilest, knowing all is well.

All may be well, or it may not be, but we must read this reassuring conclusion with a sympathetic seriousness that has been earned by other lyrics, if we are not to find it insipid. The last stanza recalls a moment in section LXXXV when the poet also imagined that he heard a whisper from beyond, saying " 'Tis hard for thee to fathom this; / I triumph in conclusive bliss, / And that serene result of all." It *is* hard to fathom, and the inertness of the language reveals that Tennyson has not fathomed it either and has no inward acquaintance with this mood of bliss. What is more, the poet knows this, and these lines from LXXXV are followed by the stanza that I have already quoted as an instance of his nervous and careful honesty: "So hold I commerce with the dead; / Or so methinks the dead would say . . ." Tennyson can hardly have intended these intimations of reassurance from the beyond to strike us as insipid, but he clearly did intend to confess their vulnerability to the charge of mere wishfulness and willfulness.

I have discussed in chapter 1 the often-quoted conclusion of section CXXVIII—"I see in part / That all, as in some piece of art, / Is toil cöoperant to an end"—and made there the relevant point that this faithful conclusion is quite unconnected to anything else in the lyric. The poet sees what he sees only "in part," and the human future that section CXXVIII in fact imagines is not progressive or meaningful at all, but trivial and monotonous. Although this vision of monotony is explicitly cast as a challenge to meaning and progress, and although the poet makes clear that this is not the version of the future that he believes in or reasons from in this lyric, he imagines no other, and this leaves his closing answer to the challenge a mere and unsponsored assertion.

It is true that assertion need not be mere assertion, and wishfulness need not be mere wishfulness. Indeed, the wish is logically and doctrinally equivalent to the human will and desire that acquire, in other late lyrics of *In Memoriam*, a virtually creative power. But what Tennyson and his poet feel with real conviction and express with real power, as *In Memoriam* approaches its end, is not a faith in God or in the external arrangements of history, and these faiths do seem merely wishful because they are set forward so clearly as the expected and approved solution to an observed problem. It is true that the poet expects and approves this solution himself, and I do not mean that his beliefs in God and man are mere impositions upon him or that they are insincerely professed. I do mean that his faith in God finally depends on a prior faith in himself, in the authority and vitality of his own imagination and feeling, and that this faith, though by no means unshakable, is the strongest and deepest the poet of *In Memoriam* has, as measured by the power and frequency and lack of reserve with which it is expressed. Even the unreserved and almost heretical exaltation of human love and of Arthur Hallam, in the closing lyrics of *In Memoriam*, depends on an act of transformation and possession that is, first and last, the poet's own, proud act.

The poet himself does not always seem to recognize this, however, and this is especially true when he looks back over his poem. He has been reading himself in many of these late lyrics and telling over his story in a variety of ways, even when he seems, as in section CXVIII, to be describing the history of the earth. Section CXXIV was another version of the story, an attempt to infer the workings of divine providence from the poet's own course of recovery. But it is the recovery itself, the subjective experience of that recovery, that actually gets dramatized in section CXXIV and in the rest of *In Me-*

moriam. And, as the self-examination of earlier lyrics has demonstrated, the poet is more apt to resist than to celebrate the evidences of his own progress, always preferring to discover in himself a deep constancy and an unwavering devotion to his friend. In section CXXV, the poet's mission, as in many earlier lyrics, is to acknowledge and then to explain away his past inconsistencies of tone and statement. But the reading of his own, recorded past produces a different and more satisfying mixture of qualities than can be found in his readings of the imagined human future or than he, perhaps, intends.

> Whatever I have said or sung,
>   Some bitter notes my harp would give,
>   Yea, tho' there often seem'd to live
> A contradiction on the tongue,
>
> Yet Hope had never lost her youth;
>   She did but look through dimmer eyes;
>   Or Love but play'd with gracious lies,
> Because he felt so fix'd in truth:
>
> And if the song were full of care,
>   He breathed the spirit of the song;
>   And if the words were sweet and strong
> He set his royal signet there;
>
> Abiding with me till I sail
>   To seek thee on the mystic deeps,
>   And this electric force that keeps
> A thousand pulses dancing, fail.

This revisionist account of the earlier sections of *In Memoriam* can hardly expect to be believed. At most, it would win from us the suspicious and conditional assent that we offer to what is possible, but not plausible or finally arguable. When Hope looks with dimmer eyes, how can she prove her identity? Perhaps Love breathed the spirit of lyrics full of care, but how can the identity of an anonymous and lying author be established? This is another of the faiths that cannot be proved, but it can be challenged, nevertheless, because it makes assertions not about heaven or the future, but about linguistic events in which we, as readers, have participated. And I think that most readers will find it implausible that Love and Hope are the self-assured authors of all that has come before.

For one thing, we have seen this argument before, but with different names. In section XVI, it was not Love, but a constant and personified Sorrow who expressed herself variously and thus merely appeared to be inconstant. In section LXXXVIII, the poet played a harp that he could not quite control and that expressed an obscure and more plausible mixture of joy, grief, woe, and glory. Affirming his constancy in these varying ways, the poet gives evidence of change, and the exchange of muses, the substitution of Love for Sorrow, remains unexplained. Even within this lyric, the mixture of Hope and Love is a complication that could grow into yet another version of self-contradiction.

What truly abides in the poem is the urge that all these lyrics spring from, the urge to explain away contradiction and change, and another, more primal, urge or power that keeps generating these changes and moving the poet forward. This could be time or God or history, but the poet feels it within himself and he names it here as "this electric force," the energy source that compels the poet outward and forward in spite of himself and that is the true focus of this lyric, in spite of itself. The achieved and memorable mixture of qualities in this lyric is not the mixture of Love and Hope the poet points back to, but the mixture of life and death, vitality and enervation, in the last stanza. The poet sails out across the deeps that a temptingly allied image would plunge him into—section CVIII turned away from the "depths of death," but this lyric knows they are unavoidable—and the electric and vital force persists and prolongs the pulse of the stanza as long as it can—but fails, with the last, inevitable word.[10] The celebration of Love, the new orthodoxy that the poet intends to establish, passes over into a subdued chant of homage to "this electric force," the one power whose existence the poem surely confirms. This is a power of movement, a vital force directed forward and outward, but always sensed within.

In the last three lyrics of *In Memoriam*, the poet rises in confidence and joy to make several different statements of faith, each one carefully circumscribed, all of them together setting the final terms of his belief. The "electric force" of CXXV returns as the "living will" to which section CXXXI is addressed, a generalized human will that the poet invokes on behalf of the species. But sections CXXIX and CXXX are addressed to Hallam and express in the first-person singular the achieved and idiosyncratic faith of the poem. In section CXXIX, the poet wants to establish the connection between his love for Hallam and his faith in a divinely ordered cosmos, but he mingles the two kinds and objects of his devotion in a language that blurs both:

> Dear friend, far off, my lost desire,
>   So far, so near in woe and weal;
>   O loved the most, when most I feel
> There is lower and a higher;
>
> Known and unknown; human, divine;
>   Sweet human hand and lips and eye;
>   Dear heavenly friend that canst not die,
> Mine, mine, for ever, ever mine;
>
> Strange friend, past, present, and to be;
>   Loved deeplier, darklier understood;
>   Behold, I dream a dream of good,
> And mingle all the world with thee.

It is not clear from this lyric why Hallam should be loved the most when the poet feels there is a lower and a higher, nor is it clear from past lyrics that this really is so. The poet wants to make clear that his love of this man is not at odds with a love of God, but the weak paradoxes of the second stanza link the human and the divine by evoking neither with any particularity or conviction. In the last line of the stanza, the poet hugs something to his breast with a moving and wondering insistence that mingles the tones of a child and a lover. But insisting is not persuading, and what this line captures is not Hallam but the pathos of desire. The last stanza gets closer to the authentic and peculiar facts of the poet's relationship to his lost friend. This friend is "strange" now, as well as "sweet" and "dear," and the unexpected adverbs of the second line are emotionally rich and right, as the inert paradoxes of the second stanza were not.[11] But after this, the stanza just trails away. The intransigent privacy of "dream my dream, and hold it true," from section CXXIII, has become a public display here—"Behold"—of an approved product, "a dream of good." And the last line announces a mysterious and miraculous accomplishment, without at all helping us to imagine it.

That job falls to section CXXX, and it turns out that the poet needs no ethical categories and only a single and unintegrated mention of God to explain a dream of mingling that is once again private and fantastic.

> Thy voice is on the rolling air;
>   I hear thee where the waters run;
>   Thou standest in the rising sun,
> And in the setting thou art fair.
>
> What art thou then? I cannot guess;
>   But tho' I seem in star and flower
>   To feel thee some diffusive power,
> I do not therefore love thee less:
>
> My love involves the love before;
>   My love is vaster passion now;
>   Tho' mix'd with God and Nature thou,
> I seem to love thee more and more.
>
> Far off thou art, but ever nigh;
>   I have thee still, and I rejoice;

> I prosper, circled with thy voice;
> I shall not lose thee tho' I die.

The terms of celebration are familiar. Diverse places and times become one, distance and absence are denied, and the rising and setting of the sun surround the lyric present and the strong self. There will be no wait here for a "far-off divine event," because the far off is ever nigh.

In its third stanza, this lyric is no clearer than CXXIX about the mixing and involving that are somehow being accomplished, but the Hallam-charged landscape of the first two stanzas is quite clear, if quite extravagant, in its portrayal of yet another act of imaginative excitement and appropriation. This is a loudly, unabashedly Romantic landscape, more clearly and particularly indebted than earlier lyrics to Romantic ways of realizing the full moment through the animation of natural appearances. Hallam dwells, like the divine presence of "Tintern Abbey," in "the light of setting suns," and the lyric draws also on the imagery and thought of the Lucy poems, especially "She dwelt among the untrodden ways," and "A slumber did my spirit seal." It draws most of all from stanza XLII of "Adonais":

> He is made one with Nature: there is heard
> His voice in all her music, from the moan
> Of thunder, to the song of night's sweet bird;
> He is a presence to be felt and known
> In darkness and in light, from herb and stone,
> Spreading itself where'er that Power may move
> Which has withdrawn his being to its own.

As section V had predicted, the poet relies at his moments of intensest feeling on the conventions that a shared tradition provides for the expression of that feeling. Although it refuses the mediation of time and other selves, this lyric accepts the mediation of other texts, a fact represented internally in its acceptance of the mediations of nature. The poet surrounds himself with meaning, with a landscape made of language, and every object in the world is empowered, like language, to sustain the presence of the dead. But these objects are also extensions of the poet's own presence, and he is so vividly and immediately connected to the world that he more than half-creates here, so sure of the imaginative survivals that he can guarantee with the power of his own imagination, that he closes, not in celebration of Hallam or the world, but with a series of strong and unqualified affirmations of the first-person singular. He never truly lost the object of his desire, but has him "still," a firm and secure act of possession. He prospers. And in the last line, "I shall not lose thee tho' I die," he predicts a triumph not only over the death of the beloved, but over the death of the self, hardly admitting, in the audacity of "tho'," that a physical death is inevitable.

Next to self-assertion and self-assurance of this purity, the affirmation of section CXXXI must seem spare and cautious. To end with CXXX would be to suggest that a mood of its intensity can be sustained, and such a suggestion would violate the character of the poem. The poet cannot hold the dream of presence and must rest content in his last lyric with contemplating the future and looking forward to what he will gain in death, rather than celebrating what he has and cannot lose. Of course, this faith in the future is itself something to be celebrated, but the terms of celebration are carefully public and qualified:

> O living will that shalt endure
>   When all that seems shall suffer shock,
>   Rise in the spiritual rock,
> Flow thro' our deeds and make them pure,
>
> That we may lift from out of dust
>   A voice as unto him that hears,
>   A cry above the conquer'd years
> To one that with us works, and trust,
>
> With faith that comes of self-control,
>   The truths that never can be proved

> Until we close with all we loved,
> And all we flow from, soul in soul.

The only circularity here is in the reasoning, which asks for a faith in the future time when faith will be justified. The circles of section CXXX have otherwise yielded to the living will, which cuts like a vector through time, and the first-person singular of the strong imagination has yielded to the first-person plural of the voice of his kind. The self now needs to be controlled rather than asserted. Voice is not a present gift to the self, but a communal aspiration, and, when it comes, it will be a cry directed merely as if at God, a God who is named vaguely and functionally as "him that hears," and the "one that with us works."

Some commentators have supposed that the "living will" was yet another of God's names in the lyric, but Tennyson corrected this mistake in several places and wrote in a notebook, "I meant it for the human Will, the strongest part of the Individuality." In the *Memoir*, he glosses the term as "Free-will, the highest and enduring part of man,"[12] but the first, more private explanation seems better. In the first stanza of CXXXI, the living will does not descend from the heights, but rises up from a place beneath and is not a choice-making faculty at all, but an animating power.

It is this power that creates faith in *In Memoriam* and that creates life out of dust. Faith in God comes second and depends upon the inward action of the human spirit. Indeed, faith is weakened and imperiled in the request "that we may . . . trust, / With faith that comes of self-control / The truths that never can be proved."[13] To "trust, with faith" is superfluous, and merely adds another breakable link to the chain. Why should faith depend on "self-control," if not because the uncontrolled self will range into all the God-excluding moods of *In Memoriam*, moods of doubt and despair, or of imaginative self-sufficiency? The poet's celebration of religious faith is a celebration of the power of his own will and imagination to create faith and to believe in their own creation.[14] *In Memoriam*, taken all together, finally and most forcefully celebrates this power for itself. The poet makes and expresses himself in *In Memoriam*—not a portrait of Arthur Hallam and not a doctrine of any kind—and his emotional recovery is a healing and directing of the power of self-assertion that he has displayed from the first.

EPILOGUE

At the close of section CXXXI, the poet's narrative is finished. Although Tennyson did not distinguish the Epilogue to *In Memoriam* by giving it that title, he did separate it clearly from the sequence of stanzas that has come before by giving it no number at all. And when he says in the third stanza that he has numbered "some thrice three years" since "that dark day" of Hallam's death, he deliberately violates the internal chronology of *In Memoriam* and steps outside the seasons of the poem to place himself in 1842, nine years after Hallam's death, and the year of Cecilia Tennyson's wedding to Edmund Lushington. Closing his poem in celebration of this wedding, Tennyson likened it to "a sort of divine comedy—cheerful at the close." But it is someone else's wedding, after all—his own took place only when *In Memoriam* was completed and published—and Tennyson keeps stepping in and out of the festivities, a reluctant and brooding celebrant for whom "cheerful" is never quite the right word, even in the resounding optimism of his conclusion. I admire the end of the Epilogue too much to regret its privilege of place, but it is important not to extend this privilege automatically and uncritically and to be swept by the closing rush of feeling into overestimating the actual conclusiveness of this conclusion. Tennyson may have set the Epilogue apart from all that precedes it, but it is audibly and recognizably the expression of a particular moment, not a separated commentary on the history of moods, but a mood-piece of its own.

That mood is admittedly hard to place through much of the Epilogue, and Tennyson alternates between stately self-regard, honeyed celebration, rueful withdrawal, and the peculiar awkwardness that he reserves for his notations of the mundane. When he joins bravely in the spirit of the celebration, although thinking inevitably of Hallam, his assurance that "My drooping memory will not shun / The foaming grape of eastern France," is ludicrous rather than poignant. And when he observes the "maidens of the place / That pelt us in the porch with flowers," it is in a language that turns real events into unreal pictures, but makes no magic in the process.

The Epilogue becomes verbally exciting only when Tennyson's own mood is transformed by the events of the happy day and when that mood in its turn sweeps and transforms the landscape in a sudden surge of feeling.

> Now sign your names, which shall be read,
> Mute symbols of a joyful morn,
> By village eyes as yet unborn;
> The names are sign'd, and overhead
>
> Begins the clash and clang that tells
> The joy to every wandering breeze;
> The blind wall rocks, and on the trees
> The dead leaf trembles to the bells.

The issues and the language of section XCV return here, as the poet moves from a consideration of the simple fact that writing outlives writers into a suddenly full-voiced testimony to the animating influence of the excited human spirit. Celebrating the marriage of others, this voice celebrates itself, and it is imagination as well as love that remakes the blind and dead world.

This sequence of feelings is characteristic of the Epilogue—a moment of quiet reserve, held for a beat, and then swept up in an access of feeling and movement. There are passing emotional flutters:

> A shade falls on us like the dark
> From little cloudlets on the grass,
> But sweeps away as out we pass
> To range the woods, to roam the park . . .

And there is, most memorably, the powerful surge of feeling at the close, the beautiful and powerful language that emerges out of the poet's solitude and out of the silence after bell-ringing ceases:

> Again the feast, the speech, the glee,
> The shade of passing thought, the wealth
> Of words and wit, the double health,
> The crowning cup, the three-times-three,
>
> And last the dance;—till I retire:
> Dumb is that tower which spake so loud,
> And high in heaven the streaming cloud,
> And on the downs a rising fire:
>
> And rise, O moon, from yonder down,
> Till over down and over dale
> All night the shining vapour sail
> And pass the silent-lighted town,
>
> The white-faced halls, the glancing rills,
> And catch at every mountain head,
> And o'er the friths that branch and spread
> Their sleeping silver thro' the hills;

I have interrupted this remarkable sentence, which occupies the last eleven stanzas of the poem, in mid-career. It reins itself in to "touch with shade" and with "tender gloom" the happiness of the new-lyweds and then breaks out again to range higher and wider than the moonlit landscape, to take in the sounding ocean and the whole night sky, with "star and system rolling past." The poet's own imaginative mobility matches the heaving animation of the cosmos, and, as in his earlier moments of imaginative excitement, he allies himself with the forces of nature, enjoying the easy and certain sense of power that comes of commanding the moon to rise and the future to come. In the last, very often quoted, stanzas of his poem, Tennyson rouses himself to expect more of the future than just that it will come. He looks forward to the perfection of the species, celebrating marriage and generation; he looks backward one last time to Arthur Hallam, whose own perfections of person made him a noble type of the wondrous species to come; and he looks outward from Hallam to God:

> That friend of mine who lives in God,
>
> That God, which ever lives and loves,
> One God, one law, one element,
> And one far-off divine event,
> To which the whole creation moves.

In quoting these lines once again, I wish only to emphasize how reliant they are on the emotional and verbal momentum of the stanzas that precede them and how readily that crucial, penultimate line may collapse into wistfulness. The far-off divine event is very far off indeed, so far off and vague, in fact, as to be unimaginable and unimagined. Tennyson can hardly claim without further explanation that his reunion with Hallam is the justifying end of the whole creation, and yet no other future event has been so excitedly set before us. On any orthodox reading, it must be the events of the book of Revelation to which the line looks forward, and yet there is no suggestion here of judgment and no suggestion in orthodox doctrine of the evolution of a "crowning race." As so often in *In Memoriam*, imaginative energy is invested not in portraying the future, but in evoking the present-tense satisfaction of a state of aroused expectation.

As sober prediction, the last stanzas simply make no sense and have no basis. Tennyson never pretends to have seen much empirical evidence of the progress of the species, and he does not pause to sort out any of the difficulties that attend on identifying Hallam with the "crowning race" of the distant future. This is a race

> . . . that, eye to eye, shall look
> On knowledge; under whose command
> Is Earth and Earth's, and in their hand
> Is Nature like an open book;

a race whose virtues are more like the poet's own, in his most exalted and vaunting moments, than like any of the descriptions that we have read of the wise and pure-spirited Hallam. The poet is swept up in a grand feeling at the close of the Epilogue, and this is what gives the language and the lyric their life, but it is also the sign that he is not a removed commentator, that he has not settled finally into a secure and hopeful vision of human events, but has simply managed once more to rouse himself to a state of excited satisfaction. He speaks, as always, from the moment, and from the evidence of his own imaginative experience.

Neither as it unfolds lyric by lyric nor as it lives in memory does *In Memoriam* conform to any of the shapely forms that it occasionally borrows from religion or science or literary convention. These are rather the background against which it defines itself, out of which the poem and the poet's self emerge. The critic's search for literary analogues parallels the poet's search for appropriate and comforting models for his own experience. Both can yield aids to understanding, but neither, ultimately, can do more than confirm the uniqueness of what it seeks to describe. Even structural models that are specific to *In Memoriam*, whether dividing it into four parts or nine or more, fail to organize it satisfactorily, because they cannot encompass groupings that have no respect for sequence. Section VII belongs as surely with section CXIX as with sections VI and VIII. A moment of consciousness that can feel itself to be the single true moment can also expose linear duration as a fiction, and declare its truest affinity with any of the accumulated data of memory. It need not respect an arbitrary chronology, just as the reader need not respect the admittedly arbitrary chronology of *In Memoriam*. And I suspect that most readers do, in fact, dispense with this chronology by reading around in the poem far more often than they read through it and by remembering best its moments of most powerful self-expression, regardless of their place in its sequence.

And yet, arbitrary or not, the order of the poem is there for us, as Tennyson's achievement and the poet's discovery. Change exists, in spite of all grief-drunk or ecstatic witness to the contrary, and it is one of the chief aims of *In Memoriam* to rationalize this change and to write a history that makes sense of the poet's movement from grief to something else. In order either to write history or to make sense, the poet must learn to accept and exploit the betrayals of time and language. He has turned language to account by discovering in the form of his poem the true image of his situation in time: of a past that is fixed and still and yet constantly altered by the addition of new moments to it; of a present that is always in the making, half made and half discovered. He chooses and creates the present, one word at a time, but he can create the present only out of the past, and his choice is constrained by both the form and the feeling that are his recorded legacy. If the strict laws of the *In Memoriam* stanza are an emblem of the poet's own obsessive repetitions of feeling, the freedom and flexibility that he finds for himself within this stanza are at once an aesthetic and a spiritual achievement. The imaginative force to which the poem bears witness is a force that presses both forward and outward, from one moment to the next, and, at each moment, from the poet to the reader.

It is thus the strength and changeability of his own "imaginative woe" that the poet comes finally to accept and to celebrate and whose existence *In Memoriam* most surely confirms. I doubt that Tennyson himself would have endorsed the terms of this conclusion or found much comfort in them. There is always something tricksy and unsatisfying in the forms of triumph over death that the imagination is said to offer, and there is ample biographical evidence that Tennyson both wanted and found an orthodox faith in the immortality of the soul. I do not think, however, that *In Memoriam* can give us this faith, or that Tennyson thought it could, either, and his poem never tires of confessing that its faith in God is provisional and ultimately groundless. But neither do I think that *In Memoriam* simply and finally offers us the deconstruction of its faiths in God or man or the strong imagination. Indeed, it is because of the obsessive self-questioning of the poem, because a deconstruction of the poet's faith is all too easy, that it will not satisfy. Once we have shown that the poem calls in question all its own affirmations and undercuts all its own professions, we are left only with a new and mild orthodoxy, the affirmation of irony, agnosticism as dogma. But it is no more the poem's skepticism than its faith that finally secures its value. We could have looked elsewhere for the demonstration, in the blandly oracular words of "The Ancient Sage," that "nothing worthy proving can be proven." But we can find only in *In Memoriam* the particular form of this poet's experience in time. The sovereignty of time and the chanciness and vulnerability of any affirmation are amply and repeatedly acknowledged by the argumentative waywardness of the poem and by the self-contradictory variety of its moods. But something is affirmed, nevertheless, by the success with which the poem sustains the identity of the poet, from one mood and moment to the next, and thus represents the self-justifying motion of persistent and imaginative life.

NOTES

NOTES TO PREFACE

1. McLuhan's essay first appeared in *Essays in Criticism* and is reprinted in *Critical Essays on the Poetry of Tennyson*, ed. John Killham (London: Routledge and Kegan Paul, 1960).

NOTES TO CHAPTER ONE

1. In *The Ordinary Universe* (New York: Macmillan, 1968), p. 97.

2. [Hallam Tennyson], *Alfred Lord Tennyson: A Memoir* (London: Macmillan, 1897), I, 305.

3. All citations from *In Memoriam* are from the edition of Susan Shatto and Marion Shaw (Oxford: Oxford University Press, 1982). Hereafter cited as Shatto and Shaw.

4. Although I keep the poet and the author carefully distinct, I have not hesitated to call the poet's friend "Hallam"—as he does not hesitate to call him "Arthur." Nothing is lost by this identification, and it helps to keep down the elegant variations on "his friend," "his lost friend," "his beloved friend," etc.

5. *Memoir*, I, 304.

6. "*In Memoriam*," in *Selected Essays* (New York: Harcourt, Brace and Co., 1950), p. 291.

7. *Tennyson* (New York: Macmillan, 1972), p. 214. Although I am here setting my own views in contrast to those of Mr. Ricks, I must gratefully acknowledge a large debt to his work on Tennyson, both to the critical book I have cited and to his superb edition of Tennyson's poems. He is the critic of Tennyson with whom I have most often been engaged in mental conversation in the writing of this book.

8. *The Poetry of Experience* (New York: Random House, 1957), pp. 35-36. Alan Sinfield also cites this passage in *The Language of Tennyson's "In Memoriam"* (Oxford: Basil Blackwell, 1971), p. 26.

9. *Westminster Review*, October 1855. Quoted in Ricks, *Tennyson*, p. 221.

10. James Kincaid, *Tennyson's Major Poems* (New Haven: Yale Univ. Press, 1975), p. 109.

NOTES TO CHAPTER TWO

1. For interesting analyses of the formal means by which this calm is achieved see Reuben Brower, *The Fields of Light* (New York: Oxford University Press, 1962), pp. 33-34; W. David Shaw, *Tennyson's Style* (Ithaca: Cornell University Press, 1976), pp. 141-42; Alan Sinfield, *The Language of Tennyson's "In Memoriam,"* pp. 1-7.

2. *A Commentary on Tennyson's "In Memoriam,"* 3rd ed. (London: Macmillan, 1910), p. 96.

3. *Complete Works* (New York: Harper and Bros., 1860), IV, 432. I am grateful to Barbara Harman for referring me to this passage.

4. The offending lines were "For her feet have touched the meadows / And left the daisies rosy." For Tennyson's indignant self-defense—he planned to mail a rosy daisy to Ruskin—see the *Memoir* by Hallam Tennyson (New York: Macmillan, 1897) I, 511.

5. *A Map of Misreading* (New York: Oxford University Press, 1975), p. 150.

6. This line of interpretation is strengthened by reference to the original manuscript reading of the last line: "In all his words without a plan." Ricks, ed., *Poems of Tennyson* (London: Longman, 1969), 878.

7. See *The Language of Tennyson's "In Memoriam,"* pp. 213-15, where Alan Sinfield uses section XVI as an example of analogical syntax.

8. *Works* (London: Macmillan, 1908), III, 229.

9. "Patterns of Morbidity: Repetition in Tennyson's Poetry," in *The Major Victorian Poets: Reconsiderations*, ed. Isobel Armstrong (London: Routledge and Kegan Paul, 1969), p. 9. Dodsworth is paraphrasing a passage he has just quoted from Wordsworth's 1800 note to "The Thorn."

10. Dolores Ryback Rosenblum makes just this distinction in her interesting essay "The Act of Writing in *In Memoriam*," in *Victorian Poetry*, 18 (1980), 121.

11. *Sartor Resartus* (New York: Odyssey Press, 1937), p. 219.

12. Ibid., p. 222.

13. On Tennyson's self-borrowings, see Ricks, *Tennyson*, pp. 298-312; on his borrowings from Hallam, see ibid., p. 230; and on all the kinds of Tennyson's allusions, see Ricks's essay "Tennyson Inheriting the Earth," in *Studies in Tennyson*, ed. Hallam Tennyson (London: Macmillan, 1981), pp. 66-104.

NOTES TO CHAPTER THREE

1. For FitzGerald's charges of self-indulgence, made in a letter to W. B. Donne, see Ricks, *Tennyson*, p. 214.

2. As the poet knows in section LXVII. Tennyson may merely have been ignorant of the circumstances of Hallam's burial when he wrote XXI. He was mistaken, for instance, about the route followed by the ship bearing Hallam's body, and he visited Clevedon only after his marriage in 1850. Still, when he wrote XXI, he probably knew the facts, since two possible allusions, to the Chartist movement of 1838-39 in lines 15-16, and to the 1846 discovery of Neptune in lines 17-20, suggest a late date for its composition.

3. *Selected Essays*, p. 292.

4. On "those high offices," Christopher Ricks devastatingly remarks "oh,

those." Tennyson, p. 239. See also James Kissane's remarks on section LXXV in *Alfred Tennyson* (Boston: Twayne, 1970), pp. 77-78.

5. *The Language of Tennyson's "In Memoriam,"* pp. 145-46.

6. See, for instance, Sinfield, *The Language of Tennyson's "In Memoriam,"* pp. 146-47; Kissane, *Alfred Tennyson*, p. 68; Ricks, *Tennyson*, pp. 228-29.

7. *A Commentary on Tennyson's "In Memoriam,"* p. 119.

8. He comes closest in sections XXII and XXXIV.

9. For Swinburne's criticism and Ricks's endorsement of it, see Ricks, *Tennyson*, pp. 222-23.

10. "Tennyson Inheriting the Earth," in *Studies in Tennyson*, ed. Hallam Tennyson, p. 83.

NOTES TO CHAPTER FOUR

1. *A Commentary on Tennyson's "In Memoriam,"* p. 29.

2. *The Poems of Tennyson*, p. 939.

3. *Memoir*, I, 320.

4. As noted by A. Dwight Culler in *The Poetry of Tennyson* (New Haven: Yale Univ. Press, 1977), pp. 183-84.

5. See, for instance, Alan Sinfield, "Matter-Moulded Forms of Speech," in *The Major Victorian Poets*, ed. Isobel Armstrong, pp. 62-63.

6. His note appears in his own *Works* (London: Macmillan, 1908), III, 252.

7. The others are XXII, XXX, LVIII, LXXVIII, LXXXVII, and CIII. Of these only LXXXVII and CIII stay in the past tense and do not shift over to the "now" of utterance.

NOTES TO CHAPTER FIVE

1. Quoted in Shatto and Shaw, p. 258.

2. A point made more fully by Alan Sinfield in *The Language of Tennyson's "In Memoriam,"* pp. 137-38.

3. Shatto and Shaw quote from the letter in their notes to this section. For the full text, see *The Letters of Arthur Henry Hallam*, ed. Jack Kolb (Columbus: Ohio State University Press, 1981), pp. 784-86.

4. *Memoir*, II, 474

5. *Tennyson's Major Poems*, p. 107.

6. See Michael Mason's comment that "the consolation achieved at the end of *In Memoriam* has several aspects, but it consists chiefly in the mourner's ability to mourn or, more precisely, to state his loss without being intolerably distressed by it." He goes on to remark of section CXIX in particular that "the mourner is not learning to find Hallam (any more than he finds him with any certainty in lyric XCV) but learning to lose him." "The Timing of *In Memoriam*," in *Studies in Tennyson*, ed. Hallam Tennyson, pp. 162, 163.

7. Quoted in Ricks, *Tennyson*, p. 226. The letter to Alexander Baillie is dated 10 September 1864 and appears in *Further Letters of Gerard Manley Hopkins*, ed. Claude Colleer Abbott (Oxford: Oxford University Press, 1938).

8. The most troublesome of the new loose ends is the probable dating of these lyrics, since it seems likely that CXXII was written before the others and thus would have had a hard time alluding to them. And yet it might easily have alluded to the moods out of which they were written. The dating, furthermore, is quite uncertain.

9. William Allingham, *Diary* (1907), p. 288, 8 August 1880. Cited in Ricks, *Tennyson*, p. 277.

10. Although the "this" of "this electric force" seems to me to make certain the inwardnesses of the experience, I am puzzled by the thousand pulses that it keeps dancing. A thousand is an oddly small number for the scrupulous Tennyson to use in reference to all of humanity, but too large to refer to anything else. One almost expects to discover an obscure doctrine that imagined the creation of souls in batches of a thousand.

11. I am indebted to Christopher Ricks's comments on these lines in *Tennyson*, pp. 223-24.

12. Cited in Shatto and Shaw, p. 291.

13. Alan Sinfield in *The Language of Tennyson's "In Memoriam,"* p. 69, quite plausibly links "self-control" with the "strength and grace" that the poet strives for in a manuscript version of the stanza, but this does not make less peculiar or noteworthy the linkage of "faith" and "self-control" in the stanza we have.

14. In their notes to section CXXIV of *In Memoriam*, Susan Shatto and Marion Shaw quote a fascinating passage from a letter of Arthur Hallam to Tennyson: "With respect to prayer, how am I to distinguish the operations of God in me 'from motions in my own heart'?" In the last phrase, Hallam is apparently quoting from Tennyson's own phrasing of the question. He goes on to answer: "Why should you distinguish them? or how do you know there is any distinction?"

INDEX
TO SECTIONS OF
IN MEMORIAM

INDEX
TO
PERSONS

PRINCETON ESSAYS IN LITERATURE

LIBRARY OF CONGRESS CATALOGING-IN-PUBLICATION DATA

Peltason, Timothy, 1951-
 Reading in memoriam.

 (Princeton essays in literature)
 Includes index.
 1. Tennyson, Alfred Tennyson, Baron, 1809-1892.
In memoriam. I. Title. II. Series.
PR5562.P44 1985   821'.8   85-42698
ISBN 0-691-06650-7 (alk. paper)